Ireland's Comfort Food
& Touring Attractions

Ireland's
Comfort Food
& Touring Attractions

❧

Viki Pidgeon

Acknowledgments

Thank you Barney, my husband, for driving from county to county and town to town during our "Irish holidays". Barney, when talking of our travels, fondly refers to this as "Driving Miss Viki".

A hundred thousand thank yous are in order for Steven Roberts of Heritage Island. Steven allowed me to include pictures of various touring attractions as well as the order form for the "Essential Touring Guide", at a reduced price.

An ever-so-grateful thank you to my sister, Barbara Heintz, for the many hours spent creating the cover of my book. I love it!

A special thank you to Eric Taylor for his expertise in the world of publishing. Eric always made time to talk with me and answer loads of questions.

Many thanks to Pat Prather for the excellent work on the book layout and design.

Much appreciation goes to Martha Keen, a long lost, recently found roommate from my college days at Western Kentucky University. Martha is my proofreader.

Thank you George Graham for testing recipes. George grew up in the restaurant business and is right at home in the kitchen.

Contents

A small sampling of "the Forty Shades of Green"

Introduction

MY DREAM is to someday have a small apartment, (or nest as I often refer to it), in Ireland. It was during my first visit that I fell in love with Ireland, its land, and its people; for some inexplicable reason I felt I was supposed to be there. Ever since that holiday in 1998 I wake up and fall to sleep thinking and dreaming about Ireland and how I might go about making my dream come true. Who knows, maybe this Irish cookery book will be the answer to my prayers.

Recipes included in *Ireland's Comfort Food & Touring Attractions* have been shared by the chefs and proprietors of restaurants, hotels, country houses, tourist attractions, and castles throughout the Emerald Isle. Bia na Mara and Board Bia have been kind enough to grant me permission to include a few of their delectable recipes, as have the famous Murphy Brewery, Durrus Farmhouse Cheese, Odlums, and the Connemara Smokehouse. Had it not been for the spirit of sharing, this book would not have become a reality. Each and every day I am grateful for the generosity of the busy chefs that took the time to share their mouth-watering recipes. And surprisingly, the dishes are easy enough for the everyday cook to prepare, a big plus for the majority of us.

WHEREVER YOU GO, whatever you do, comfort food awaits you. Comfort foods may vary from country to country but they all seem to have one thing in common: they make you feel good. So what exactly is comfort food? The answer to this question hinges on your own personal taste, what kind of mood you are in, who you are with or where you are; the weather can even play a roll in determining what is comfort food. What may be comfort food for one person may not be for the next. But one thing for sure, comfort food seems to have a soothing effect on people. On a cold winters day a piping hot bowl of soup may give you that warm, fuzzy feeling. A particular food may bring back fond memories of childhood. Remember when Mom made chocolate chip cookies and you got to lick the bowl? Then, the anticipation as the cookies baked, the aroma filling the kitchen and finally sitting down to a plate of warm cookies and a glass of milk. Oh yes, life was good. And let's not forget the old-fashioned favorites like meatloaf, shepherd's pie, Irish stew, and the quintessential favorite macaroni and cheese. I have never met a person who doesn't like a good mac and cheese. Not only do you derive satisfaction from eating comfort food, there is also great pleasure in the ritual of creating it. Stirring a big pot of soup, stew or chowder on a cold, dreary day may be just what the doctor ordered.

There is no shortage in Ireland when it comes to this particular food category. On the following pages you will find an array of yummy soups, hearty stews, gorgeous chowders and mouth-watering casseroles to fill your very soul. The recipes have been shared by the chefs of the Emerald Isle. Why not put on your apron, find that large pot, and start creating your own comfort zone?

Soups

**Book bags line the railing at Kylemore Abbey International Girls'
School as the day students wait for the school bus.**

I WILL ALWAYS remember our visit to Kylemore Abbey and Garden. Built by Mitchell Henry in 1868, it was known as Kylemore Castle. In 1920 Kylemore Castle was sold to Benedictine nuns fleeing Belgium during World War I, and the castle became an Abbey. While touring the Abbey I spotted one of the nuns seated at an old antique desk, reading a book. She looked to be in her nineties, and she was there to answer any questions a visitor might have, and I had quite a few. I learned that there are 17 nuns living in the Abbey, as well as the girls who attend school there. How amazing! Never did I dream that Kylemore Abbey housed an international girls' school. As if the news of a private girls' school weren't enough of a surprise, there was something else in store. Out of the blue, singing filled the air. It was as though I had just arrived in Heaven. The girls, I assume, were in choir practice. There is also a beautiful Neo-Gothic Church, walled garden, pottery studio, crafts shop, and restaurant on the grounds. Plan to spend a few hours – it is very picturesque and relaxing.

Tomato & Basil Soup

⋮

14-ounce can of plum tomatoes
6 fresh tomatoes
2 ribs celery, finely chopped
3 medium carrots, peeled and chopped
2 medium onions, diced
2 tablespoons tomato puree
5 cups vegetable stock
½ teaspoon ground coriander
1 tablespoon brown sugar
4 cloves garlic
3 tablespoon Worcestershire sauce
dash of Tabasco sauce
2 tablespoons dried basil
salt and pepper to taste
cream, optional

Place all ingredients, except the basil, salt, pepper, and cream, in a saucepan and cook for 30 minutes. Blend the soup at low speed with a mixer. Add salt, pepper, and basil, stir gently. If desired, add cream to taste.

Kylemore Abbey & Garden
KYLEMORE, CONNEMARA
CO. GALWAY

Roasted Squash Soup with Basil Pesto

1 butternut squash
small amount of olive oil, to brush inside
of halved squash
6 cloves garlic, in their skin
4 shallots/1 medium onion, finely chopped
4 cups vegetable stock
1/8 teaspoon salt
juice of one lemon

Pesto:
1 clove garlic, peeled
2 handfuls fresh basil
4 tablespoons pine nuts
4 ounces Parmesan cheese, freshly grated
5 tablespoons olive oil
salt to taste

Preheat the oven to 375 degrees. Cut the squash in half using a large knife, (be careful as the skin can be very tough), and remove the seeds. Place the squash halves on a baking pan with the garlic. Brush the inside of the squash with a little olive oil. Place the squash and cloves of garlic in the oven for 30-40 minutes, or until very tender. Remove from the oven and allow squash to cool. While the squash is in the oven prepare the pesto. Put all the pesto ingredients in a food processor and blend briefly until it becomes a rough textured sauce. Taste and adjust the seasoning if necessary. Once cool enough to handle, scoop out all the flesh of the squash and place in a large pan with the finely chopped shallots. Peel the roasted garlic and add the pulp to the pan. Add the stock and salt. Bring to a boil and simmer for 10 minutes. Remove from the heat and allow soup to cool slightly. Blend the soup in batches until smooth. Return the soup to the pan and add the lemon juice a little at a time, tasting after each addition. Serve the soup with a dollop of pesto.

Belle Isle School of Cookery
LISBELLAW, ENNISKILLEN
CO. FERMANAGH

Our ever-so knowledgeable, ever-so patient, fun-loving
teacher, Chef Liz Moore of the Belle Isle School of Cookery.

IN NOVEMBER OF 2005 I enrolled in the month-long diploma class at the Belle Isle School of Cookery, scheduled to begin in September of 2006. Finally the day had arrived, and on a beautiful Saturday afternoon my husband Barney and I navigated our way onto the Belle Isle Estate, located in the beautiful, lush county of Fermanagh in Northern Ireland. We soon found Charles, resident manager of Belle Isle Estate, who welcomed us and handed me the key to the apartment that I would be calling home for the next month. Barney and I had the apartment to ourselves, as my roommates had not yet arrived. We explored the estate and dined in Carrybridge, a small village about 2 miles away before turning in for the night. Sunday morning we awoke to the mooing of approximately 75 resident cows, which would become my new alarm clock.

One by one the cookery school students were arriving. Sofia and Hannah arrived together, since they are the best of friends and had signed up for cookery school together. When the two made their entrance, Barney and I were napping. He would soon be leaving Belle Isle to drive to Dublin and then wing his way homeward the following day. Our naptime was interrupted by the noises coming from the ground floor. First we heard the door to the apartment open and close, then each and every door on the ground floor was opened and closed. We could hear them oohing, aahing and happily chatting away. Barney woke up saying, "I think your roomies have arrived." Pretty soon the two were tromping up the stairs, once again opening and closing each door they passed. My bedroom was at the very end of the hallway and the only door that had not yet been flung open – it was just a matter of time. Sofia opened the door and was totally shocked to see Barney lying in bed. Her eyes were sooo BIG as she told Barney (with her hands over her mouth) how sorry she was for bursting into the room. I don't think she even saw me in the other bed. Poor girl. She probably thought she had a 60-year-old, silver-haired man for a roommate. With Hannah directly behind her she quietly closed the door. The two of them together couldn't keep from giggling as they scurried down the hall, flew down the stairs and ran out the door they had entered only a few short minutes before. We could still hear them laughing outside. And that is how I met the two Scottish lasses that I would be sharing the apartment with during my stay at Belle Isle.

Hannah and Sofia, two of my giggly "roomies" proudly display their risen bread dough.

Roasted Carrots, Parsnips & Ginger Soup with Herb Croutons

3 medium-size carrots, peeled and cut into chunks
3 medium-size parsnips, peeled and cut into chunks
4 ounces fresh ginger, peeled and cut into chunks
2 bay leaves
1 tablespoon chopped rosemary
3 tablespoons extra-virgin olive oil
1 medium-size onion, peeled and sliced
2 tablespoons grape seed oil
1 teaspoon garlic puree
3 quarts cold water
1 tablespoon vegetable bouillon paste or 2-3 cubes
salt to taste
white pepper, freshly ground
herb croutons

Preheat oven to 360 degrees. Place carrots, parsnips, ginger and bay leaves in a baking tray. Sprinkle with rosemary and olive oil and roast in the oven for about 45 minutes or until well roasted. In a large saucepan, over high heat, sauté onion with grape seed oil and garlic. Leave for about 5 minutes. Add roasted vegetables and cold water. Cover saucepan and bring to a boil, skim bubbles and add vegetable bouillon paste. Turn heat to medium and cook for about 45 minutes. In a blender liquidize the soup and pass through a medium fine sieve. Season to taste. Serve with herb croutons

St. Clerans Manor House
CRAUGHWELL
CO. GALWAY

THE WEE, STORYBOOK-LOOKING village of Adare is a little piece of Heaven. Adare boasts an array of places to see and things to do. You will find Desmond Castle, The Franciscan Friary, The Trinitarian Priory, The Augustinian Priory, stone buildings and thatched cottages. Some of the thatched-roofed cottages are hundreds of years old. Try your luck at fishing the River Maigue, a favorite pastime of fishermen from near and far. Perhaps you are a horse lover. The Clonshire Equestrian Centre and the Adare Manor Equestrian Centre should fill the bill. And we mustn't forget the Limerick Racecourse if you are of the betting nature

Photo courtesy of Heritage Island.

Tomato & Roast Pepper Soup

3-4 tablespoons butter
2 medium onions, peeled and chopped
2 pounds fresh tomatoes, chopped
2 tablespoons tomato puree
3 potatoes, peeled and sliced
1 ½ pints chicken stock
2 large red bell peppers, roasted, skinned and cut into pieces
salt and pepper to taste

Melt butter; add onions and fry gently. Add tomatoes, tomato puree, potatoes and stock. Simmer for about 45 minutes. Season the soup with salt and pepper. Process the soup in a blender. Lastly, stir in the bell pepper pieces.

Serves 6.

Dovecot Restaurant
ADARE HERITAGE CENTRE
ADARE
CO. LIMERICK

My friend George tested this recipe in the middle of February, a time of year when fresh tomatoes aren't all they should be. He used high quality, canned whole tomatoes. Because they had juice added, he used 28-ounce and 14-ounce cans and drained off the excess juice.

Lentil & Ham Soup

Day before:
3 cups lentilles de Puy, soaked overnight in cold water*

2 tablespoons olive oil
3-4 tablespoons butter
1 large onion, roughly chopped
4 carrots, roughly chopped
1 white leek, roughly chopped
3 stalks celery, roughly chopped
2 cloves garlic, finely chopped
6 slices of smoky bacon, roughly chopped
salt and pepper to taste
3 cups lentilles de Puy (soaked overnight in water)
9 cups chicken stock

Pour the olive oil into a large Dutch oven, add the butter and cook on medium low heat until the butter has melted. Add the chopped vegetables and chopped bacon, and turn the heat to medium. Sauté until the onions are transparent. Add salt and pepper to taste. Cover and turn heat to medium low, continue cooking until carrots have softened. Add the soaked lentils to the vegetable mixture and pour the chicken stock over the top. Replace the lid and bring to a boil. Reduce heat and allow the mixture to simmer gently, stirring occasionally, until the lentils are cooked, (about 30 minutes). Allow soup to cool for a further 30 minutes. Blend the soup until very fine and pass through a sieve. Add more salt and pepper if needed. Heat to desired temperature to serve.

*Lentilles de Puy, the French green lentils from the village of Puy, in the Auvergne.
Seeing as though Puy is a little ways away I substituted regular lentils found at my local grocery.

Rathsallagh House Hotel & Golf Club
DUNLAVIN
CO. WICKLOW

NEWCASTLE WEST is just a few miles south of Adare. As I mentioned earlier, I would love to buy an apartment in Ireland. You can't imagine how excited I was when I learned that Guinness was conducting a "Win your Own Pub in Ireland" contest. The year was 1999, the pub was J. O'Sullivan's, located in Newcastle West, Co. Limerick. J. O'Sullivan's was pictured on the entry form, which I had picked up at my local bottle shop. In Ireland liquor stores are referred to as bottle shops. The pub was perfect; this I could see from checking out the picture, with the aid of a magnifying glass. Best of all, there were living quarters above the pub. I submitted no less than 30 entries, feeling certain I would be one of the 10 lucky finalists competing for the keys to the pub. Unfortunately I didn't win the pub, nor was I one of the finalists, such a huge disappointment. A lady from Portland, Oregon was the lucky winner. I would have to defer my dream of an apartment in Ireland a bit longer.

Barney and I have since visited the pub on two separate Irish holidays. On our first visit I longingly admired the colorful stained glass windows of the numerous Guinness advertisements created over the years. The framed newspaper article featuring the "Win Your Own Pub in Ireland" contest, along with the pub winner's picture was displayed in a prestigious spot close to the bar area.

Farney Castle, co. Tipperary, home to Cyril Cullen and family.

Apple and Tomato Soup

⁙

2 cups water
2 Bramley's Seedling Apples, peeled cored and sliced*
1 Karmijn de Sonnaville apple, peeled, cored and sliced*
2 pounds fresh, ripe tomatoes, halved
2 cloves garlic, peeled
salt and pepper
1/3 cup extra virgin olive oil
1 tablespoon tomato puree
1 teaspoon caster sugar
2-3 basil leaves, chopped
Salt and freshly ground black pepper, to taste

Put the water, apples, tomatoes and garlic into a large saucepan and season with salt and pepper. Cover with a tight fitting lid and bring to a boil over a medium heat. Turn heat down and simmer for about 20 minutes, by which time the apples, tomatoes and garlic should have broken up. Add the remaining ingredients. Use a hand-blender to puree soup to desired consistency. Add more salt and pepper to taste.

*Bramley's Seedling apples and Karmijn de Sonnaville apples are popular cooking apples grown in Europe.
In America the Granny Smith apples would be a good substitute.

The Apple Farm
CAHIR
CO. TIPPERARY

Spicy Parsnip Soup

3-4 tablespoons butter
4 ½ cups vegetable stock
½ pound potatoes, peeled and roughly chopped
3-4 ounce onion, peeled and roughly chopped
½ pound parsnips, peeled and roughly chopped
2 cloves garlic, peeled and chopped
1 tablespoon pepper
1 tablespoon hot curry powder
½ cup cream
salt

Put butter and vegetable stock in a large Dutch oven. Add the potatoes, onion, parsnips and garlic, and bring to a simmer. Allow vegetables to simmer until they are soft. Add the pepper and curry powder and stir. Allow the soup to cool down a little. Blend the soup in batches in a blender or food processor until smooth. Return the soup to the pan and stir in the cream. Add the salt to taste and gently heat through.

Bunratty Castle and Folk Park
BUNRATTY
CO. CLARE

Bunratty Castle & Folk Park
Photo courtesy of Heritage Island

BUNRATTY CASTLE and Folk Park would be an outstanding attraction to visit with children, as visitors can see characters depicting 19th century life in an authentically re-created 19th century village. The castle, built in 1425, and has undergone a massive restoration in 1954, bringing it back to its original splendor. Had you not arrived by way of modern transportation, you would think you had traveled through time. Medieval banquets are held in the castle from May to October. Visitors can dine at the banquet by simply making a reservation. This is an ideal place to visit on your way to or from the Shannon Airport, which is a short six and a half mile drive.

JAMES J. MURPHY and his three brothers founded Murphy Brewery in 1856. James the eldest of the four grew the company for its first forty years. At that time a brother and his sons took over the day-to-day running of the brewery. Eventually the Heineken Group became involved, and Murphy's brand became a part of Heineken in 1983. Murphy's is available in 70 countries. Not only are Murphy's Stout and Murphy's Red enjoyable libations, but they also add a distinctive flavor when used as a cooking ingredient. Why not try this recipe and see for yourself?

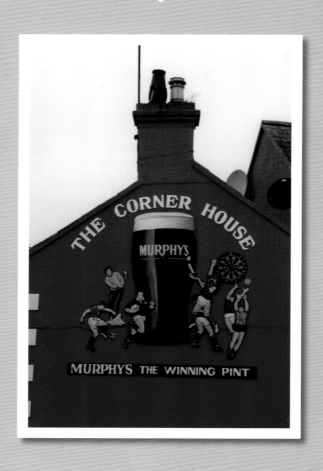

Grandma Murphy's Broccoli & Blue Cheese Soup

❧

1 onion, chopped
1 pound broccoli, chopped
1 large zucchini, chopped
1 large carrot, peeled and chopped
1 medium potato, peeled and chopped
2 tablespoons butter
1 ounce sunflower oil
8 cups vegetable stock or water, divided
salt and pepper
3 ounces bleu cheese

Put onion, broccoli, zucchini, carrot, potato, butter, sunflower oil and stock or water into a large saucepan. Heat the ingredients for about 5 minutes, stirring well. Bring to a boil. Add salt and pepper to taste, cover the saucepan and simmer gently for 25-30 minutes. Strain the vegetables and retain the remainder of the liquid. Puree the vegetables in a food processor or blender. Return the pureed vegetables and the remainder of the liquid to the saucepan. Bring the soup back to a gentle boil and stir in the cheese until it melts. Care should be taken to ensure the soup does not boil quickly as this will make the cheese stringy.

Murphy Brewery
CORK

My friend George also tested this recipe, and he added a chopped clove of garlic. He also grated nutmeg over the top of each bowl of soup.

Wicklow Broth

1 turnip, peeled and chopped
8 medium carrots, peeled and chopped
1 head celery, washed well and chopped
3 leeks, washed well and chopped
2 large onions, peeled and chopped
1 bay leaf
1 gallon cold vegetable stock
1 pound pearl barley
½ pound garden peas
½ cup parsley
salt and fresh ground black pepper, to taste

Place chopped, turnips, carrots, celery, leeks, onions and bay leaf in a large pot and pour cold vegetable stock into the pot. Bring to a boil, turn heat down and simmer for 45 minutes. Skim the broth throughout the entire cooking process. Add the barley and simmer for an additional 30 minutes. Three minutes before serving, add the peas and parsley, (no sooner or they will loose their color). Season broth with salt and freshly ground black pepper.

Avondale House and Forest Park
RATHDRUM
CO. WICKLOW

BEFORE WINGING your way to Ireland it would be wise to figure out approximately how much cash you will be needing, and what the current exchange rate is. It is also important to know the exchange rate for Northern Ireland as well as the Republic of Ireland, if your travels will include Northern Ireland. There is a total of 32 counties, 26 are in the Republic of Ireland, with the remaining 6 in Northern Ireland. The Republic of Ireland is on the euro, while Northern Ireland is on the pound, (United Kingdom pound). If you have access to a computer, simply key in currency converter or exchange rate, key in the appropriate information, and the current exchange rate will appear. Now then, if you will be arriving in Ireland on a Sunday or national holiday you have two options as far as having the proper currency on hand goes. First, you can have a local bank in your hometown convert money for you, or you can convert money in the Irish airport you fly into. Also keep in mind that many of the Bed & Breakfasts are not set up to take charge cards, so don't count on charging your room.

While touring Killarney you are bound to see horse-drawn buggies.
A lovely way to take in the clean fresh air and view the countryside.

Chilled Apple and Tomato Soup

12 ripe plum tomatoes cut into small pieces
6 Granny Smith apples, peeled, cored and cut into small dice
2 ¼ cups apple juice
2 ¼ cups tomato juice
12 basil leaves
2 ¼ cups stock syrup
extra basil leaves for garnishing

Place the tomatoes and apples into a large bowl. Reserve some chopped tomatoes and chopped apples for garnishing. Pour the juices and stock syrup into the bowl, and add the basil. Blend with a hand blender until smooth. Pass through a fine sieve. Refrigerate until needed. Garnish each bowl or cup of soup with finely chopped tomatoes and apples and a basil leaf.

Park Hotel Kenmare
KENMARE
CO. KERRY

DO YOU PLAN ON driving around the Ring of Kerry? If so plan on spending the night or a few hours at the very least in Kenmare. Kenmare is a beautiful town with lots of restaurants and shops and it is at the beginning of the Ring of Kerry. The 5 Star Park Hotel Kenmare is an extraordinary place and holds more awards than I can list. Fine dining, a small movie theatre, and a spa are just a few of the many amenities at this luxurious hotel.

Cream of Celeriac & Brandy Soup with Crispy Pancetta

2 tablespoons butter
2 garlic cloves, chopped
1 medium onion, skin removed and diced
2 heads celeriac, chopped
2 ounces brandy
8 ¾ cups chicken bouillon
4 ½ cups cream
pancetta strips, crisped in the oven, for garnish
truffle oil for garnish

Melt the butter in a heavy soup pan. Add the chopped garlic and onions, sauté. Add the chopped celeriac and cook for 5 minutes until soft. Flambé with brandy, add the chicken bouillon and cream, and bring to a boil. Reduce heat and simmer for 15 minutes. Blitz soup (blend in a blender in batches) until smooth. Pour into heated bowls and garnish with pancetta strips and truffle oil.

Stonebridge Restaurant
RICHHILL
CO. ARMAGH

Stonebride Restaurant is the proud winner of the Northern Ireland
Tourist Board Hospitality Award for 2006.

This bright red letter box can be found at the entrance of the Belle Isle Estate, which is home to the Belle Isle School of Cookery.

Sergio and his lovely wife Sarah "testing the cheese"

✻

GAVIN, HEAD CHEF and owner of Scoffs Restaurant shared his recipe for Yellow Courgette & Blue Cheese Soup, a name I love. Courgettes are what we in America know as zucchini, and the word itself simply sounds beautiful to me. Gavin couldn't have been more enjoyable to talk with about my forthcoming book. After telling him the book would be exclusively soups, stews, chowders and casseroles, he replied, "Oh comfort food!"

Yellow Courgette & Cashel Blue Cheese Soup

3-4 tablespoons unsalted butter
1 ¾ pounds yellow courgettes (squash), sliced
2 cups peeled, chopped shallots
3 cloves garlic, crushed
1 ¼ cups medium chopped celery
1 ¼ cups sliced leak (white part only)
¾ pound peeled potatoes, sliced
½ teaspoon thyme, chopped
6 tablespoons plain flour
6 ½ cups good chicken stock
1 cup double cream
salt and pepper
10 ½ ounces Cashel Blue cheese, cubed

Melt butter in a large, thick-bottomed pan. Add the courgette slices, shallots, garlic, celery, and leaks. Sauté for about 3-4 minutes not allowing vegetables to color. Add sliced potatoes and allow to cook an additional 2 minutes. Add thyme and stir the flour into the vegetable mixture, stirring until a roux forms. Add the chicken stock, bring to a boil and simmer for 20-30 minutes. Add half of the cream and all of the Cashel Blue cheese. Bring the mixture back to a boil and remove from the heat. Season soup with salt and pepper. Ladle into bowls and finish each with a swirl of the remaining double cream.

Gavin serves homemade chunky whole meal bread with this lovely soup.

Scoffs Restaurant
ENNISKILLEN
CO. FERMANAGH

Murphy's Leek and Potato Soup

4 tablespoon butter, divided
2 leeks, chopped
1 small onion, finely chipped
¾ pound potatoes, peeled and chopped
2 ½ cups vegetable stock
salt and pepper
1 ¼ cups Murphy's Irish Red Beer

Heat 2 tablespoons butter in a large saucepan, add the leeks and onion. Cook gently, stirring occasionally, for about 7 minutes. The leeks and onion should be soft but not brown. Add the potatoes to the leeks and onions in the saucepan. Stir occasionally for 2-3 minutes. Add the vegetable stock and bring to a boil. Cover the saucepan and simmer gently for 30-35 minutes, until the vegetables are very tender. Add the salt and pepper to taste. Add the remaining butter and the Murphy's Irish Red Beer. Simmer for 2 minutes. Serve.

Murphy Brewery
CORK

Murphy Brewery

Carrot & Orange Soup with Coriander Cream

1 orange
2 1/2 tablespoons oil
3-4 tablespoons butter
1 ½ pounds carrots, finely sliced
½ bunch celery, finely sliced
1 small onion, peeled and finely sliced
1 leek, white part only, finely sliced
½ ounce fresh ginger, peeled and finely sliced
1 large clove garlic, crushed and chopped
½ teaspoon salt
½ teaspoon pepper
1 large potato, peeled and sliced
4 ½ - 6 ½ cups chicken or vegetable stock

Remove the zest of the orange and set aside. Remove skin and any white pith from the orange and set aside. Heat a large pot to medium-high and add the oil and butter. When the butter has melted add all the sliced vegetables, orange zest and garlic. Add salt and pepper. Turn down the heat and allow the vegetables to gently sauté for about 30 minutes, stirring occasionally. Doing this will allow the vegetables to release their natural juices. When the vegetables and the carrots have softened add the sliced potato. Add enough stock to cover the vegetables about 1-inch. Turn up the heat and bring the soup to a boil. Turn down and simmer the soup until the carrots and potatoes are thoroughly cooked through. In a blender or food processor, puree the soup, (you may have to do this in batches). Pass through a sieve to remove all the fibers left by the celery and leeks. Check for seasoning and the orange flavor. If more orange is required or desired add the juice of the orange.

Recipe continued on next page.

Coriander Cream:

½ cup whipping cream
5 sprigs of coriander

Finely chop the coriander leaves with a sharp knife. Add chopped coriander to the cream. Whip cream until soft peaks appear. Heat soup, ladle into a bowl and add a nice dollop of the Coriander Cream.

Rathsallagh House Hotel & Golf Club
DUNLAVIN
CO. WICKLOW

Cream of Cauliflower Soup with Julienne of Smoked Salmon with Dill

1 tablespoon olive oil
3 knobs of butter, (6 tablespoons)
4 medium-size leeks, (white parts only), chopped
1 medium-size onion, peeled and chopped
salt
finely ground pepper
1 large head cauliflower, green leaves removed, chopped
½ of a medium-size potato, peeled and thinly sliced
5 cups chicken or vegetable stock
pinch of fresh grated nutmeg
2/3 cup of cream
julienne of smoked salmon
fresh dill, chopped

In a large saucepan heat the olive oil and the butter. Add leeks and onion; lightly season with salt and pepper, and sauté slowly. Add chopped cauliflower and sauté again. Add sliced potato and pour stock over, (stock should cover the vegetables). Bring to a boil, reduce the heat and simmer slowly until cooked, about 30-40 minutes. Let mixture cool a little before putting it in a food processor or blender; blend until smooth. Pour through a wine strainer. Return soup to the pan and heat until hot. Correct seasoning if necessary, using more salt, freshly ground pepper, and fresh grated nutmeg' add the cream. Serve in warm soup bowls. Garnish with julienne of smoked salmon and chopped dill.

Park Hotel Kenmare
KENMARE
CO. KERRY

Bacon, Courgette and Cashel Blue Soup

A little olive oil
5-6 slices bacon, chopped
1 onion or 2-3 shallots, chopped
1-2 large courgettes, sliced*
2-3 large potatoes, peeled and chopped
5 cups stock, homemade if possible
3 ounces Cashel Blue cheese, or Chetwynd Irish Blue, crumbled
2/3 cup cream
black pepper
2-3 tablespoons parsley, finely chopped

Sauté the bacon for a few minutes in a little oil. Remove a few pieces of bacon for final garnish. Add the onion, courgette (reserve some slices for final garnish), and potatoes. Cover the pan and allow vegetables to cook until they are soft. Stir in the stock and simmer for 10 minutes. Remove from the heat. *Process the soup. Return to the saucepan. Stir in the cheese and cream and just heat gently. Add the reserved bacon pieces and courgette slices for final garnish. Finish with lots of black pepper and parsley.

*Courgette is the French term for zucchini
*Process the soup (blend soup in a blender until smooth).

Recipe courtesy of Bord Bia Irish Food Board.

Pear & Parsnip Soup

4 tablespoons butter
1 onion, finely chopped
pinch of salt
2 carrots, peeled and thinly sliced
1 pound parsnips, peeled and sliced
2 ounces fresh ginger, peeled and grated
2 ripe, fresh pears or 14-ounce can
1 teaspoon coriander seeds, crushed
zest of 1 orange
6 cups chicken or vegetable stock
1 cup fresh orange juice
salt and pepper to taste
sour cream for serving
fresh tarragon to garnish

Heat the butter in a large saucepan over medium heat. Add the onion with a pinch of salt and stir; allow to cook 2-3 minutes. Add the carrots, parsnips, ginger, pears, coriander seeds and orange zest. Stir well and cook for 2-3 minutes; then add the stock. Turn up the heat and bring to a boil. Reduce the heat and simmer with a lid on for 25-30 minutes, until the vegetables are very tender. Blend the soup in batches in a blender or food processor until very smooth. Return the soup to the pan and add the orange juice. Add salt and pepper to taste. It may be necessary to add a little water if the soup is thicker than you like. Serve hot with sour cream and fresh tarragon.

Belle Isle School of Cookery
LISBELLAW, ENNISKILLEN
CO. FERMANAGH

The Old Schoolhouse, Derryharney Co. Fermanagh is now a lovely private residence.

Pat O'Doherty, Mr. Black Bacon himself, smiling as usual.

Pea Soup with Black Bacon

1 large onion, chopped
3-4 tablespoons butter
4 ½ cups of bacon stock (made from dried bacon trimmings)
1 medium potato, peeled and cubes
1 pound fresh or frozen peas
salt and pepper to taste
4 thin slices of streaky black bacon, fried

Sauté the onion in the butter until translucent; add stock and bring to a boil. Add the potatoes and simmer for 10 minutes. Add peas; cook for 5 minutes. Puree the soup; season with salt and pepper and garnish with streaky black bacon.

O'Doherty's
ENNISKILLEN
CO. FERMANAGH

ANNA MARIE, one of the ladies in my Belle Isle School of Cookery, invited me to her home in Crossdoney, Co. Cavan for the weekend. Upon my acceptance she informed me that her house would be quite noisy (this I already knew) since she and her husband Gerard were the parents of 4 young children. They were wonderful hosts, thoughtful in every way. Anna Marie had bought a lovely red wine, which I am particularly fond of, for our Friday night libation. We had sampled the wine during a presentation at cookery school, so I knew it was something to be savored. After the little ones had gone to bed, Anna Marie, Gerard and I sipped the wine and talked up a storm. I'm not sure in what order that occurred but I think you have the general idea. Anna Marie sipped on a single glass of wine throughout the course of the entire evening because she would soon be the mother of five! The next morning we prepared a tasty breakfast with the breakfast sausages she had purchased from Pat O'Doherty's in Enniskillen, Co. Fermanagh. The sausages curled up a little during cooking, which is a very good thing for sausages to do. A little tidbit we had learned on a class field trip to Pat's shop. I won't get into the whys…just take my word for it. They were delicious and curling is a good thing! By the way, did I mention that I won the sausage-making contest during our visit to Pat O'Doherty's? Yes indeed, I was the proud winner of a few sausages.

Ireland's weather makes growing pretty flowers easy, even for those of us without a green thumb.

IN THE SUMMER of 1951, during the filming of *The Quiet Man*, electricity came to Cong. The wee village of Cong was featured in the movie quite a bit, especially a local pub, which is still in operation today. The townspeople were happily dancing in the streets at the prospect of having electrical power, that is until they found out they had to pay for it. Upon hearing this unwelcome news they concluded they didn't need or want electricity, and to get rid of it.

Many of the local townspeople were in the film as extras, particularly in the brawl scene toward the end of the movie. *The Quiet Man* starred John Wayne as Sean Thornton and the beautiful Maureen O'Hara as the headstrong Mary Kate Danaher. The story of The Quiet Man was written by Maurice Walsh and published in 1933 in the *Saturday Evening Post.* John Ford, the director, bought the screen rights for $10.00.

Barney and I inherited our very own tape of the movie, which I have watched countless times.

⁛

DAVID AND DIANE SKELTON pay close attention to making their home your "home away from home". They are attentive to your every need. Diane takes her cooking to the next level by using the freshest ingredients available, creating dishes that look like works of art.

Garden Pea and Bacon Soup

Butter
Olive oil
2 onions, peeled and roughly chopped
1 stick celery, chopped
1 leek, washed and chopped
3 strips lean smoked bacon, chopped
2 ½ cups chicken or vegetable stock
2 potatoes, peeled and diced
1 pound garden peas, fresh or top quality frozen
1 bouquet garni made with fresh thyme, mint, parsley, rosemary and a bay leaf
salt
freshly ground black pepper to taste
1 tablespoon cream
fresh chopped parsley for garnish
crispy bacon bits for garnish

Melt the butter in the olive oil and gently sauté the onion, celery and leek until Translucent; then turn up the heat a little and add the bacon and cook for a few minutes. Gradually add the stock and bring to a boil. Add the peas and potatoes and bring the soup back to a boil; add the bouquet garni, salt and pepper, and simmer gently for about 15 minutes, until the potatoes are soft. Remove the pan from heat, remove the bouquet garni and pour half of the soup into a blender and blend until smooth. At this point you can either blend the other half and mix the two together, or mix the blended half into the unblended half for a chunkier soup. When you are ready to serve the soup, simply add the cream and bring the soup to the consistency you like, and gently reheat. Adjust the seasoning and serve, garnished with fresh chopped parsley and crispy bacon bits.

Ballywarren Country House
CONG
CO. MAYO

Strokestown Co. Roscommon
Photo courtesy of Heritage Island

Margaret's Easy Spinach & Potato Soup

6-8 medium-size potatoes, peeled and diced
1 large onion, peeled and diced
salt
pepper, freshly milled to taste
small bunch of parsley, chopped
5-6 cups vegetable stock or water
2 handfuls spinach, washed and roughly chopped
½ cup fresh cream
pinch of nutmeg
additional cream for serving
additional chopped spinach for serving

Put potatoes, onions, salt, pepper, parsley and stock into a large saucepan. Bring to a boil and simmer until potatoes are almost cooked. Add the spinach, and cook for 4-5 minutes, and stir well. Check and adjust seasoning if necessary. Add the cream and nutmeg. If the soup is a little thick, thin with water. To serve garnish each bowl with cream and chopped parsley. Wholesome brown, bread or cheese scones are the suggested breads to serve with this tasty soup.

*Note: This recipe also works very well with broccoli in place of the spinach, along with chopped toasted almonds.

Strokestown Park
STROKESTOWN
CO. ROSCOMMON

Cashel Blue & Celeriac Soup

2 tablespoons unsalted butter
1 tablespoon olive oil
2 onions, peeled and roughly chopped
1 pound celeriac, peeled and roughly chopped
3 ¾ cups chicken stock
freshly milled black pepper, to taste
2/3 cup cream
4 ounces Cashel Blue cheese, rind removed and cubed
chives, snipped for garnish
croutons for garnish

Heat the butter and oil in a large pan and fry the onion and celeriac over a gentle heat for 3-4 minutes to draw out the flavors. Add the chicken stock, black pepper and bring to a boil; then reduce heat and simmer for about 30 minutes until the vegetables are tender. Liquidize or puree in a blender until smooth. Return soup to the pan, reduce the heat and add the cheese, stirring continually until the cheese melts. Add the cream and reheat gently. Serve sprinkled with snipped chives and croutons.

The Kilcoran Lodge Hotel Restaurant
CAHIR
CO. TIPPERARY

CASHEL BLUE is a semi-soft blue cow's milk cheese. It is unique, Ireland's first farmhouse blue cheese, made entirely on the dairy farm of Jane and Louis Grubb near Cashel in Co. Tipperary Ireland. While some milk is purchased, the majority of the milk comes from the pedigree Friesian dairy herd on the farm. The cheese is made from pasteurized whole milk. It is sold in many specialty outlets in the U.K., America and Ireland, as well as listed by most of the British Multiples. Much of the cheese is sold young, while it is firm and crumbly, but for a fuller flavor, it is best eaten at about 3 months of age, when it has a softer texture and more mature flavor. To learn more about this special cheese visit their website, www.cashelblue.com.

Louis Grubb, pictured on the left, gathering his cows together for a milking session.

Garden Vegetable Soup

1-2 tablespoons olive oil
2 tablespoons butter
1 onion, peeled and finely chopped
2 carrots, peeled and finely chopped
2 parsnips, peeled and finely chopped
2 potatoes, peeled and finely chopped
1 stalk celery, chopped
2 leeks, finely chopped
salt and pepper to taste
4 ½ cups vegetable or chicken stock
handful of pearl barley
fresh parsley or thyme
cream or dry sherry, optional

Heat a little olive oil with a knob of butter in a large pan. Add all the vegetables and cook gently for 1-2 minutes. Season the soup with salt and pepper. Add the stock and bring to a boil. Reduce to a simmer and add the barley. Cook until the vegetables are tender. Add the parsley or thyme and serve.

*For a variation on this easy to prepare soup add cream or dry sherry for extra flavor.

Belle Isle School of Cookery
LISBELLAW, ENNISKILLEN
CO. FERMANAGH

**I couldn't resist snapping a picture of this unique mosaic tile bench
in Sligo Town.**

PEOPLE ASK: what is it about Ireland that you like so much? Well, that's an easy one…everything! Actually, what appeals to me most is that everyday life turns at a slower pace. It just doesn't seem to be as hectic as it is here in America. Which reminds me, the people of Ireland refer to the United States as America, which makes me think of days gone by. So, since the Irish refer to the United States as America, I do too. I want so much to be all about anything and everything Irish. America also sounds so patriotic.

The people of Ireland are a welcoming people, so friendly and kind, down-to-earth, and genuine. The land is scenic. Rock walls, harbor towns, mountains, fields full of grazing sheep, salmon jumping in streams, churches with old stained glass windows, and of course, castles all come to mind when I daydream about Ireland. Did I leave out pubs? A huge oversight on my part, since the pub, or poor man's university, as some affectionately refer to it, is an integral part of Irish life.

You will find photos of everyday sights as well as short stories about my travels throughout Ireland with my husband Barney, and accounts of my solo adventures. The recipes are delectable and sure to please you. A few recipes from the Belle Isle School of Cookery, a lovely estate where I spent a month studying the art of Irish cooking, are also included. Enjoy!

Beef Bacon and Bean Soup

8 ounces dried white beans (haricot)*, soaked overnight
1 tablespoon oil
2 ounces streaky bacon, diced
8 ounces shin beef, diced
1-2 bay leaves
2-3 teaspoons ground cumin
1 large onion, finely chopped
3 cloves garlic, chopped
2-3 sticks celery, chopped
2 carrots, chopped
4 ounce tin* tomatoes
2 tablespoons wine vinegar
5 cups water
salt and black pepper
6 slices bread, toasted with slices of farmhouse cheese for garnish

Rinse the beans. Cover with water and boil for 10 minutes. Drain and rinse again. Heat the oil in a large pot and sauté the bacon, beef, bay leaves, cumin, onion, garlic, celery and carrots. Add the beans, tomatoes, vinegar, water and seasoning. Bring to a boil. Reduce the heat, cover and simmer for 1½ hours. Serve topped with a slice of the bread and melted cheese.

*Haricot beans are known as navy beans in America.
*tin (can)

Recipe courtesy of Bord Bia Irish Food Board

Stews

Guinness Beer Stew

⁙

½ cup onion, diced
½ cup celery, diced
½ cup ounces leek, diced
½ cup ounces carrot, diced
4 tablespoons butter
1 pound beef, diced
pinch mixed herbs, (thyme and rosemary)
½ cup flour
9 cups beef stock
2 tablespoons gravy browning, (such as Kitchen Bouquet or Gravy Master)
salt and pepper to season
1 1/8 cups Guinness

Sauté all vegetables in the butter for 5-6 minutes. Add the diced beef and cook for 5-6 minutes. Add the herbs and then the flour. Add beef stock slowly over heat while stirring; cook for another 5-6 minutes. Add gravy browning and seasoning. Slow cook for 1-1 ½ hours. Finish by stirring in ½ pint of Guinness.

Serves 8-10.

*The Guinness Storehouse Chef suggests serving this stew with champ potato and roast carrot and parsnip

Guinness Storehouse
DUBLIN

GUINNESS, the world famous black stout! It wasn't until my first visit to Ireland that I was introduced to Guinness. I was told that Guinness was an acquired taste, and I acquired it quickly. My husband Barney, Barney's dad, Barney's sister Mickey and her husband Jerry and I had the good fortune to be treated to a private tour of St. James Gate on a sunny day in May. After winding through the exhibits, we found ourselves in the bar area and naturally, we drank a few pints of Guinness. As mentioned, we visited St. James Gate and the Guinness Storehouse during our first holiday in Ireland; since that time a lot of remodeling has been completed. Now, at the end of the tour you will find yourself at the top of the building with a spectacular view of Dublin, along with a complimentary pint of Guinness. Yes, life is good. I am proud to say that I am a charter member of the 1759 Society and have a tastefully framed certificate to prove it! Members of the 1759 Society have an appreciation of and dedication to Ireland's most famous export, Guinness Stout.

During our holiday to Ireland in 2000 we took pictures of Guinness advertisements, this one is a favorite.

THE CURRAGH RACECOURSE is Ireland's most famous horse racing centre and is located in Co. Kildare. The Curragh Racecourse reminds me of home. Why, you ask? It just so happens that I live in horse country. Shelby County, Kentucky that is. Churchill Downs, home of the famous Kentucky Derby is about 20 miles away. I thought it might be interesting to do a comparison of the Kentucky Derby and the Irish Derby, or Darby as the Irish refer to it. Most likely those of you living in America assume that the Kentucky Derby was the first of the two to exist. If you think that, you are definitely not on the right track! The Irish Derby's first race was run in 1866, and the Kentucky Derby, or Run for the Roses, as it is often called, was first run in 1875. Another difference between the two is that the Irish Derby is a mile and a half race run on a grass track, whereas the Kentucky Derby is a mile and a quarter race run on a dirt track. The Kentucky Derby takes place on the first Saturday in May, and the Irish Derby takes place on the Sunday closest to the end of June. The Irish Derby plays host to approximately 31,000 spectators, and the Kentucky Derby, (hold on to your hat), attracts approximately 160,000 spectators. WOW! Whether you are in Ireland at the Irish Derby or in America at the Kentucky Derby, there are a few things that are a sure bet. The atmosphere feels almost electric as bets are wagered, and excitement fills the air as the horses pound their way around the track toward the finish line. The Curragh of Kildare Irish Stew is served in the clubhouse. It's a sure winner.

Kieren Fallon accepting the trophy for his winning ride atop Dylan Thomas in the 2006 Irish Derby.

Grey Swallow, winner of the 2004 Irish Derby, ridden by jockey Pat Smullen.

Curragh of Kildare Irish Stew

2 ¼ pounds Irish lamb
2 onions, peeled and roughly chopped
2 carrots, peeled and roughly chopped
½ turnip, peeled and roughly chopped
¾ pound mushrooms, sliced
1 floury potato, peeled and roughly chopped
2 ½ cups stock
2 cloves garlic, peeled and crushed
fresh parsley, chopped, to taste
fresh thyme, chopped, to taste
salt and pepper, to taste
champ, for serving

Preheat oven to 325 degrees. Wash the lamb and vegetables. Place the lamb and vegetables in a heavy pot. Add the stock, garlic, parsley, thyme and seasoning. Bring to a boil on the stovetop. Transfer mixture to a casserole dish and place in the oven for 2 ½-3 hours until meat is tender. What a winning combination!

The Curragh Racecourse
CO. KILDARE

The stew will be more flavorful if made a day or two before serving, as the flavors meld together.
*I added a few sprigs of thyme and two bay leaves.

Irish Stew

❧

2 tablespoons cooking oil
1 large onion, peeled and sliced
1 ½ pounds round steak, trimmed, fat removed, and cubed
1 vegetable cube
1 beef cube
2 ½ cups boiling water
½ pound carrots, peeled and roughly chopped
½ pound parsnips, peeled and roughly chopped
1 leek, chopped
salt and pepper to taste
1-2 tablespoons bistro gravy, amount used depends on consistency you like
potatoes, peeled and sliced thick

Heat the cooking oil at a medium heat in a large saucepan with a tight fitting lid for 1 minute. Add the sliced onions and cook until soft, about 2 minutes. Add the cubed steak and cook turning frequently until browned on the outside. Place vegetable cube and beef cube in a small bowl and add 1 pint of boiling water to mix, and pour over the meat and onion mixture. Place lid on the saucepan and simmer for 1 hour. Add the sliced vegetables to the mixture and pour in more water if necessary. Simmer for another hour or until meat and vegetables are cooked. Add salt and pepper to taste. Mix the bistro gravy in a small amount of cold water; stir thoroughly and add to stew. Bring stew back to a boil, turn down heat and simmer for 5 minutes. Add boiled potatoes.

Egan's House
DUBLIN CITY

BANK HOLIDAYS, yes, bank holidays play an important role in the planning of your itinerary. So, what are bank holidays? Bank holidays are 3-day weekends that pop up during the spring and summer. On our first visit to Ireland there were 2 bank holiday weekends, which didn't affect us, as we had room reservations in place. But, more often than not we don't have room reservations. We just count on driving through a town, and if the town looks interesting we find a room. That way we can travel at our own pace and don't have to race to the next town where we have prepaid for a room. Well… we learned the hard way how important it is to have accommodation in place if we plan to be in a "tourist town" on a bank holiday weekend. We arrived in Westport on a beautiful Friday afternoon; the streets and sidewalks were jam-packed with cars and people. Everyone seemed to be in such a festive mood. There were no rooms available at the first B&B we stopped at. No big deal we just hopped back in the car and drove on to another B&B only to find out once again that all the rooms were booked. It was at this stop that we were informed that it was a bank holiday weekend. I don't know how many places we drove to before finding a room, but we did find one, finally. We graciously took our room key, fetched a few of our belongings from the car, dropped them in our room and promptly left. We were on to Matt Malloy's, our favorite pub in Westport Town. The moral of the story is that it would be well worth your while to know when bank holidays are, particularly if you plan to visit a lot of tourist towns.

SUMMER, SPRING, winter or fall, no matter what the season, it's always a good time to visit Ireland. Just like so many places across the globe it is hard to predict the weather. One particular January was unseasonably warm; I could get away with wearing a long-sleeved shirt without a sweater or jacket. Obviously this was the exception to the rule. The point I am trying to make is that is not always raining, more often than not, it is clear and balmy. As a matter of fact, on the majority of my Irish holidays there were only one or two rainy days, during the 2-3 week holidays. That's not bad.

One of the many chefs of Ireland we met during our travels.

Spicy Guinness Lamb Stew

6 shanks of lamb, well trimmed
4 ½ cups water
salt to taste
freshly ground black pepper to taste
10 stalks celery, cut into 1-inch lengths
10 carrots, cut into 1-inch lengths
4 large onions, cut into chunks
1-15.9 ounce can Guinness
2 teaspoons curry powder
10 medium potatoes, peeled and sliced
2 packets of lamb stew hotpot mix*
1 large bunch of fresh parsley, chopped

Place lamb shanks in a large, deep saucepan, cover with water, add the salt and pepper, bring to a boil and simmer for 90 minutes. Add the celery, carrots and onion. Add Guinness and curry powder and simmer for 30 minutes. Add potatoes and continue to simmer until potatoes are cooked. (You can steam the potatoes separately and add to the stew before serving). Mix packets of lamb stew hotpot with water, and slowly add to saucepan. Add chopped parsley. Simmer for 30 minutes, occasionally checking to make sure stew is not sticking to the pan.

*Ingredients to make your own lamb seasoning mix are as follows:
1 tablespoon dried oregano
½ tablespoon crushed black pepper
¼ tablespoon bay leaf, crumbled
½ tablespoon dried basil

Charleville Lodge
DUBLIN

Avondale Irish Stew

2 pounds stewing lamb
1 bay leaf
salt
2 leeks, washed and roughly chopped
1 head of celery, roughly chopped
2 onions, peeled and roughly chopped
1 fennel, roughly chopped
1 pound potatoes, peeled and diced
salt to taste
freshly ground black pepper to taste
2 tablespoons fresh chopped parsley

Place lamb in large pot and cover with cold water; bring to a boil and strain. Place the lamb in a second pot of cold water with the bay leaf, bring to a boil, and turn heat down to a simmer. Allow lamb to simmer for ½ hour. Add the vegetables and diced potatoes. Cook on low for another ½ hour, or until lamb is tender. By this time the potatoes will have thickened the stew; if not; allow stew to simmer a little longer. Season stew with salt and freshly ground black pepper. Add the freshly chopped parsley just before serving.

*Note: cleaned, chopped carrots and parsnips can also be added. Chef Paul of Avondale House made a special note: never allow the stew to cook at a high heat; always allow it to simmer. It was also noted that the potato arrived in Ireland in the latter half of the 16th century, so prior to that barley or oats would have been used to thicken stews.

Avondale House and Forest Park
RATHDRUM
CO. WICKLOW

IN 1846 CHARLES PARNELL, one of the greatest political leaders in Irish history, was born at Avondale House. Surrounded by 500 acres of beautiful forest. Avondale House was designed by James Wyatt in 1777 in the Georgian style. Today it houses the furniture belonging to the Parnell family. James Wyatt was drawn to Georgian house designs, and it was he who planned the town of Westport in Co. Mayo. Avondale House and Forest Park is open to the public.

Avondale House
Photo courtesy of Heritage Island

GETTING AROUND IN IRELAND. Will you travel by bus, train or car? If your answer is car and you are from American you will, of course, be renting a car. What model or what color is anyone's guess. Whatever your choice it will be tricky finding your car on the street, or in a car park (parking lot) mainly because you just wont be used to it being "your car". With this in mind, I always pack antenna decorations. They are made of hard foam and attach to the end of our car antenna. This way we can easily be spot our car. One antenna decoration is a bright orange Mickey Mouse head, the other (in case someone can't live without a little orange Mickey Mouse) is a small round ball with a little cowboy hat on it. They work like a charm!

Chili Bean & Mixed Vegetable Stew

6 ounces red kidney beans, soaked overnight
2 tablespoons oil
1 onion, chopped
2 cloves garlic, crushed
1 teaspoon ground cumin
¼ to ½ teaspoon chili powder
2 tablespoons flour
2 pounds ripe tomatoes, finely chopped in a
blender or food processor
2 tablespoons tomato puree
1 vegetable stock cube

salt and pepper to taste
1 small carrot, diced
1 small potato, diced
2 celery sticks, chopped (optional)
4 ounces cauliflower florets
1 red or green bell pepper, deseeded and
chopped
4 ounces mushrooms, wiped clean and sliced
1 courgette (zucchini), sliced
For garnish: grated cheddar, sour cream or
natural yogurt and parsley

Drain the beans and cook in plenty of water until tender, about 1 hour, making sure the beans boil rapidly for at least 15 minutes. Drain. Heat the oil in a large saucepan, add the chopped onion and cook until transparent. Add the crushed garlic, cumin and chili powder and cook for an additional minute. Stir in flour and add tomatoes, tomato puree, stock cube, salt and pepper. Simmer gently for 5 minutes. The sauce should be quite thick and rich in flavor by this time. Add the carrot and potato to the sauce; cover the pan and continue to simmer for approximately 10 minutes, until the carrot is almost cooked. Add the celery, cauliflower and bell pepper, and allow to simmer for 5 minutes. Finally add the mushrooms and courgette; continue to cook, covered, until all vegetables are tender, about 5-10 minutes. Stir in the beans and allow to heat through. Garnish each serving with grated cheddar cheese, sour cream or natural yogurt and parsley.

Serves 4-6.

Drumcreehy Guest House
BALLYVAUGHAN
CO. CLARE

Irish Stew

11 cups water
2 teaspoons salt
2 ¾ pounds lean diced lamb
clove
bay leaf
1 small bunch thyme, washed
1 small bunch rosemary, washed
½ teaspoon garlic paste
25 pearl onions, peeled
6 medium carrots, peeled and cut into slices about 1/3 inch thick
18 small potatoes, peeled, steamed (potatoes should be the same size)
30 scallions, washed and blanched
salt and pepper to taste

Bring the water to a boil with 2 teaspoons of salt. Add the diced lamb and bring to a boil. Turn heat down to a simmer, skimming the stock frequently. Simmer for 5 minutes. Place the clove, bay leaf, thyme and rosemary in a small muslin bag, tie bag closed and add to the simmering stock with lamb. Continue simmering for 1 hour. Add the onions and carrots and continue simmering until the lamb is very tender. Remove the herb bag and add salt and pepper to taste. Skim off any excess fat and add the potatoes and scallions.

* Serves 6

Ashford Castle
CONG
CO. MAYO

Chowders

WHEN I STOOD on the magnificent grounds of Ashford Castle, I thought of John Wayne and Maureen O'Hara, and wondered if perhaps I might be standing on the very spot where they once stood. *The Quiet Man*, released in 1952, is the well-known award-winning movie starring John Wayne as Sean Thornton and Maureen O'Hara as Kate Danaher.

Maureen O'Hara was born in Renelagh, County Dublin. Her maiden name is Fitz Simons. During the summer of 1951 the filming of *The Quiet Man* took place in and around County Galway and County Mayo, much of it filmed in the quaint village of Cong. Director John Ford wanted the movie shot where it took place. Mr. Ford, as well as the actors and actresses, stayed at Ashford Castle. John Wayne brought his family, including his 4 children, Michael and Toni, who were teenagers at the time, and Patrick and Melinda, the two younger ones. Maureen O'Hara brought her baby and nurse.

❧

The ruins of the 12th century Monk's Fishing House. There is a hole in the floor that the monks would drop their fishing line through.

Seafood Chowder

2 medium onions, peeled and chopped
1 large carrot, peeled and chopped
1 leek, washed and chopped
4 ounces butter (1 stick)
½ cup cream flour
11 cups fish stock
3 cups mussel stock
2 cups cooking wine
3 cups cream
16 ounces mashed potatoes
9 ounces potatoes, peeled and roughly diced
1 cup finely diced carrots
1 cup finely diced fennel
1 cup cut scallions

3 teaspoons lemon juice
1 teaspoon Tabasco
2 teaspoons Worcestershire Sauce
Salt and pepper to taste
5 ounces prawns (shrimp) cooked and peeled
5 ounces mussel meat, cooked and bearded
5 ounces white fish, diced (not cod)
5 ounces salmon
5 ounces smoked salmon
1 bunch tarragon, washed, picked and sliced
1 bunch basil, washed picked and sliced
1 bunch flat leaf parsley, washed, picked and sliced
1 bunch chives, washed and cut

Sauté the onion, carrot and leek in butter until soft. Add the liquids and bring the mixture to a boil, stirring frequently, especially in the beginning. Simmer for 18 minutes. Strain through colander and return mixture to a boil, (do not blitz). Add mashed and diced potatoes, carrots and fennel, and allow soup to simmer for 5 minutes. Add all the remaining ingredients, (except the herbs), and adjust the seasoning. Do not allow chowder to cook any longer. Transfer soup to a shallow container, place in refrigerator and allow it to cool. When soup is almost cold stir in the chopped herbs and continue to chill.

*This tasty chowder is best made the day before you plan to serve it.

Ashford Castle
CONG
CO. MAYO

Everyone loves seafood! That is everyone except for those poor souls who have seafood allergies. Here's hoping that you are blessed with "the luck of the Irish" and can happily eat seafood.

Fitzpatrick's Chowder

6 ounces butter (about 1 ½ sticks)
1 small carrot, roughly chopped
green part of 1 small leek, chopped
3 shallots, peeled and chopped
2 cloves garlic, peeled, crushed and finely chopped
2 ¼ cups white wine
6 ½ cups fish stock
9 ounces salmon, cut into pieces
9 ounces cod, cut into pieces
4 ounces prawns, (shrimp)
4 ounces mussel meat, cut into pieces
2 ¼ cups cream
5 basil leaves, finely chopped
salt and pepper to taste
arrowroot to thicken, (optional)

Melt the butter in a large, heavy saucepan or Dutch oven. Add the vegetables and Garlic; sauté until softened. Add the wine and reduce by half. Add the fish stock and bring to a boil. Add the fish, prawns, and mussel meat. Turn heat down and simmer for 5 minutes. Add the cream, basil, salt and pepper, and serve. If you like a thicker consistency, add a little arrowroot to thicken.

Fitzpatrick's Bar & Restaurant
DUNDALK
CO. LOUTH

DURING OUR VISIT in 2000 Barney and I chose a Bed & Breakfast somewhere outside Limerick for our last night in Ireland. We had stayed up late, drinking more than our share of stout in the pub, which was attached to the B & B. The Irish sure do make it accommodating for those of us who like the pubs. The next morning Barney and I were chatting away with the B & B owner (her name escapes me). Exactly how we started talking about football, (known as soccer in America) is anybody's guess, but most likely there had been an important match the day before, as we were coming off a weekend. At any rate our hostess told us her boyfriend was a football player, a carry man. Well, this is when the confusion began. Barney and I couldn't figure out exactly what position a carry man would be. After asking a few questions, which most likely didn't make a lot of sense to her, we finally realized that her boyfriend was a Kerry man. That is to say, he was from Co. Kerry. We all had a good laugh at that one! After breakfast we said our thank yous and goodbyes and drove on to the Shannon Airport. It was when Barney emptied the contents of his pockets to pass through security that he found our B & B room key. On arriving back home, we did, of course, mail the key back.

John and myself in one of Ireland's walled gardens.

RUTH, EMMA AND SAM, a few of my classmates from the Belle Isle School of Cookery on a lazy Sunday afternoon at Florence Court, a splendid 18th century house and demesne* in Northern Ireland. The Cole family, known as the Earls of Enniskillen, once lived at Florence Court. There is a wonderful collection of fine Irish furniture in the main house, many of which are the original pieces used by the Cole family.

* A demesne is an estate, territory, region or domain.

Fermanagh Black Bacon & Chicken Chowder

2 tablespoons butter
1 onion, chopped
8 ounces Fermanagh black bacon or other black bacon available
2 pounds chicken breast, cut into small pieces
4 pounds potatoes, peeled and sliced
5 cups chicken stock
2 ½ cups cream, (1 pint)
bunch of fresh parsley, chopped

Melt the butter in a large skillet over medium heat; add the chopped onions and fry. Add the chopped black bacon and chicken. Fry for a few minutes. Add the potatoes, chicken stock, and cream; turn heat down to a simmer. Simmer mixture until the potatoes are cooked through. Add the parsley, and simmer a couple of minutes longer.

Florence Court
ENNISKILLEN
CO. FERMANAGH

Molly's Scallop Chowder

6 scallops, cleaned and washed
6 ounces monkfish or other firm whitefish
2 cups milk
fennel sprig
bay leaf
1 small to medium sized onion, chopped
4 ounces mushrooms, chopped

2 ounces butter
4 ounces flour
2 cups fish or vegetable stock
2/3 cup single cream
1 tablespoon white wine
bacon, cooked and chopped for garnish on individual servings

Stew scallops and monkfish gently in milk with fennel and bay leaf for about 10 minutes; cut scallops and monkfish into small cubes and set aside. Meanwhile, fry onion and mushrooms in butter and add flour to make a roux. Gradually add milk that scallops and monkfish were stewed in and the fish or vegetable stock; simmer until smooth. Stir in scallops, monkfish, and cream. When ready to serve, stir in the white wine. Top each serving with chopped bacon.

Serves 4-6.

Connemara Smokehouse
BALLYCONNEELY, CONNEMARA
CO. GALWAY

French priests on Holiday in Connemara.

EACH IRISH HOLIDAY Barney and I take requires a brand new map of Ireland. We completely wear out the maps we take on our trips, folding, unfolding, highlighting the roads we travel, and writing down miles traveled each day equals one messy, worn out map. Usually I buy the map and put it in my carry bag along with a magnifying glass. Our last holiday was no exception, once again I bought a map – and a deluxe map it was. Nice and big, which was definitely not to our advantage. It was so big that we had to get out of the car to unfold it. The whole scenario would have made for a great Candid Camera episode.

Irish Crab and Bacon Chowder

1 tablespoon butter
1 olive oil
3 strips bacon, chopped
1 large onion, peeled and sliced
1 clove garlic, finely chopped
1 tablespoon vermouth
2 ½ cups fish or chicken stock
1 large potato, peeled and diced
1 pound white crab meat
1 14-ounce can of sweet corn
sea salt to taste
black pepper, freshly ground to taste
dash of fish sauce or anchovy essence (extract)
2/3 cup cream
fresh herbs, finely chopped, marjoram, oregano, thyme, rosemary, basil and tarragon

In a large saucepan, over medium high heat melt the butter in the olive oil and fry the bacon. Turn the heat down a little and sweat the onion and garlic for a few minutes. Add the vermouth and the stock, bring to a boil and add the potato, cook until the potato is soft; then stir in the crab meat, sweet corn, sea salt, pepper and fish sauce. Cook gently for a few minutes. Add the cream and chopped herbs and continue cooking for 30 minutes.

Ballywarren Country House
CONG
CO MAYO

Scallop Chowder

∵

2 tablespoons butter
1 medium onion, thinly sliced
2 sticks celery, chopped
2 medium carrots, diced
1 large potato, scrubbed and diced
4 ounces lean back bacon, rind removed and chopped
10 fluid ounces vegetable stock
12 ounces whiting fillets, skinned and cubed
4 ounces scallops, sliced
1 ¼ cups milk
1 tablespoon cornstarch
sea salt to taste
black pepper, freshly grated to taste
fresh flat leaf parsley, chopped, for garnish

Melt the butter in a large pan; add the onions, celery, carrots, potatoes and bacon, and sauté gently until slightly softened. Pour in stock and simmer until potatoes are just tender. Add the cubed whiting and sliced scallops and simmer for 4 minutes. Blend the milk and cornstarch and add to the pan through a sieve. Season. Stir carefully until thickened. Garnish each bowl with fresh chopped flat parsley and serve.

Recipe compliments of Bia na Mara

The "Waiting on Shore" monument is in Rosses Point, Co. Sligo. The sculpture reflects the age-old anguish of a seafaring people who watched and waited for the safe return of loved ones.

Ted hamming it up with Charlie Chaplin who spent many holidays in
Waterville, Co. Kerry with his large family.

Seafood Chowder – Smugglers Style

2 pounds mussels, scrubbed and cleaned
fresh parsley, chopped
1 Spanish onion, peeled and finely chopped
1 clove garlic, peeled and chopped
¾ cup dry white wine
5 tablespoons butter
4 ounces salmon, diced

4 ounces, shrimp, peeled and cleaned
4 ounces cod, skinned, boned and diced
4 oysters, shucked, cleaned and diced
3 tablespoons flour
black pepper to taste, ground
4 tablespoons cream
fresh parsley, chopped, for garnish

Place mussels, chopped parsley, chopped onion and chopped garlic into a large, heavy pot, over a medium-high heat. Pour white wine over and add ½ ounce of the butter. Bring to a boil. Once the mussel shells open; remove them from the pot and set aside. Place the salmon, shrimp, cod and oysters in mussel stock. Bring to a simmer for 1 minute only. Strain mixture into a large stainless steel bowl and set aside, making sure to reserve the stock. Melt the remaining butter in the pot, add the flour and mix to form a roux. Pour reserved stock into the pot, mix together and simmer for 4 minutes over a medium-low heat. Remove from the heat, add the fish, shrimp, oysters and cream, (do not add the mussels). Garnish individual bowls of chowder with mussels and fresh chopped parsley.

Smugglers Inn
WATERVILLE
CO. KERRY

Salmon of Knowledge Chowder

2 onions, peeled and chopped
4 potatoes, washed and sliced
4 ½ cups vegetable stock (made from cubes)
1 pound skinless, boneless salmon, cut into chunks
2 15 ¼-ounce cans creamed corn
1 cup milk
salt and pepper to taste
2 dozen hazelnuts, shells removed and finely chopped
1 cup fresh chopped parsley

Put onions and potatoes in a large sauté pan. Pour over the vegetable stock and simmer for about 8 minutes, until the potatoes are soft, but not broken. Add the chunks of salmon and the creamed corn along with a splash of milk. Continue adding milk until the chowder is to your desired consistency. Gently simmer for 5 minutes, until the salmon is cooked through, (you want it to flake). Add salt and pepper to taste. Sprinkle the chopped hazelnuts and parsley on top of individual servings.

Serves 4

Farney Castle
HOLYCROSS
CO. TIPPERARY

FARNEY CASTLE may ring a bell, that is if you have traveled in the Holycross area of Co. Tipperary. Or quite possibly you may have a Cyril Cullen Knitwear tag on one of your favorite scarves or sweaters. You could say that Cyril Cullen has knitted his way to fame. He is an international fashion designer who loves to knit.

In 1994 Cyril purchased Farney Castle, which would become the backdrop for Cyril's knitwear collections. Buyers from across the globe travel to Holycross to see his fabulous collections, all housed in an Irish castle. As luck would have it, you too can visit Farney Castle for a guided tour. After the tour, feel free to visit the shop and take a look at the gorgeous masterpieces Cyril creates. Purchase a sweater, coat, scarf or hat, and you will be wearing a work of art.

Cyril Cullen with his daughters, Emily and Benita, modeling sweaters from Cyril's Jacob Sheep Collection.

Avondale Seafood Chowder

3 medium carrots
1 small fennel
1 small onion
4 sticks celery
1 leek
2 tablespoons butter
¼ cup Pernod
½ gallon fish stock
1 bay leaf
8 ounces skinless, boneless whiting fillet

4 ounces skinless, boneless salmon fillet
8 ounces mussels
8 ounces cockles
8 ounces shrimp, shell removed and cleaned
1 ounce carrageen moss (roux can be used)
1 cup milk
½ cup heavy cream
salt and pepper to taste
fresh chopped parsley to garnish
toasted fennel seeds to garnish

Sauté vegetables in melted butter until soft and flame with Pernod. Add stock and bay leaf and bring to a gentle simmer. Cook seafood separately in baskets lowered into stock. Cook shrimp for 3 minutes, mussels and cockles for 3 ½ minutes, and the salmon and whiting for 5 minutes. Reduce the stock and vegetable mixture by half and add the carrageen moss in a basket and simmer for ½ hour. Remove the carrageen moss and all the jelly. Flake the cooked whiting and salmon and add to the chowder, as well as the cockles and shrimp, (do not add the mussels); allow chowder to simmer for ½ hour. Add the milk and the cream, bring to a boil, and season with salt and pepper. Turn heat down to a simmer and skim off the impurities. Taste and adjust seasonings if necessary. Garnish with fresh chopped parsley and toasted fennel seeds and mussels in their shells.

Avondale House and Forest Park
RATHDRUM
CO. WICKLOW

Seafood Chowder

2 tablespoons oil
1 large onion, finely chopped
1 large carrot, finely chopped
4 sticks celery, peeled, and finely chopped
8 ¾ cups milk
8 ¾ cups cream
1 potato, peeled and diced
1 pound, 2 ounces mussel meat, cut into pieces
1 pound, 2 ounces baby prawns, (shrimp)
½ pound haddock, cut into pieces
seafood bullion
salt and pepper to taste
1 tablespoon cornstarch
Fresh Tarragon sprigs
Fresh Dill sprigs

Heat oil over a medium heat in a large, heavy saucepan. Add the onions, carrots and celery and fry until soft. Add the milk and cream and bring to a boil. Add the potatoes and cook until tender. Add the seafood and boil gently for 10 minutes. Add the bullion, salt, pepper, cornflower, tarragon, and dill. Allow mixture to thicken slightly.

Gleeson's Townhouse & Restaurant
ROSCOMMON TOWN
CO. ROSCOMMON

The Manse Restaurant at Gleeson's Townhouse offers the pure delights of quality country cooking. The name Manse is a Scottish word meaning 'minister's residence.' In 1863 the Presbyterian Church purchased the building for that purpose. Not long after it was leased to a Catholic priest, the Very Rev. Thomas D. Phillips, whom later established a national school for boys at the rear of the Manse in 1881.

Smoked Haddock & Potato Chowder

❧

3-4 tablespoons butter
½ small head of cabbage, finely shredded
3 shallots, chopped
2 large potatoes, peeled and cubed
6 ½ cups fish stock
1 pound, 2 ounces skinless smoked haddock, cut into pieces
2 ¼ cups cream

Melt butter in a large, heavy saucepan or Dutch oven. Add the finely shredded cabbage and shallots and sweat until tender. Add the potatoes and fish stock and bring to a boil; then simmer until potatoes are cooked. Add the smoked haddock and simmer for 10 minutes.

Fitzpatrick's Bar & Restaurant
DUNDALK
CO. LOUTH

Casseroles

Grace O'Malley, born into a seafaring family in Ireland in 1530, is often referred to as the "Priate Queen." This statue is on the grounds of Westport House.

❧

WESTPORT, BEAUTIFUL WESTPORT! This "Tidy Town" seems to have it all. Lovely shops, restaurants, and pubs line the streets as the Carrowbeg River lazily flows through town with its beautiful stone bridges connecting North Mall to South Mall. I suppose that you may very well be puzzled about the "Tidy Town" phrase. Ireland conducts a "Tidy Town" competition each year. Towns, large and small work hard throughout the year beautifying their towns. There's a lot of painting going on, planting of flower boxes, and decorating of shop windows. Litter is constantly being put in its place. So much so that at one point during September of 2002, there was talk about banning the sale of chewing gum in Westport. It seems that the chewing gum was showing up on the town's sidewalks creating a gooey mess. Despite the efforts to ban the product, the sale of chewing gum is still permitted. This shows to what lengths Westport will go to retain its title of "Tidy Town." Westport is now, and most likely always will be a "Tidy Town".

Boulevard Irish Chicken Dish

3 boneless, skinless, chicken breasts, cut into smaller portions
2 tablespoons olive oil
4-6 medium size potatoes, peeled and cubed
1 large onion, chopped
milk (enough for making mashed potatoes)
4 tablespoons butter
3 carrots, peeled, cut on the diagonal into thick slices
2 parsnips, peeled, cut on the diagonal into thick slices
1 small turnip, cubed
salt and pepper, to taste

Preheat oven to 325 degrees. Pan fry chicken breasts in 1 tablespoon olive oil for 10-15 minutes, turning as needed. Remove from pan and set aside. Warm the milk on a low to medium heat. Meanwhile boil the potatoes until tender. Drain potatoes and place in bowl. Add onion, milk and butter, mash together, using as much milk as needed to mash to the desired consistency, cover and set aside. Sauté the vegetables in the remaining olive oil. When vegetables are tender stir in the cooked chicken. Add salt and pepper to taste. Place chicken and vegetable mixture into the center of a shallow casserole dish, put mashed potatoes around the edge, and bake for 10 minutes.

The Boulevard Guest House
WESTPORT
CO. MAYO

Beef Casserole with Cranberries and Port

2 tablespoons flour
2 teaspoons ground mace
salt and pepper
6 ½ pounds diced chuck beef, well trimmed
3 tablespoons oil
3 large onions, chopped
4-5 cloves garlic, chopped
4-5 sticks of celery, chopped
1 tablespoon whole grain mustard
glass of red wine
glass of port
2 2/3 cups beef stock
2-3 bay leaves
2 tablespoons fresh oregano or thyme, chopped
10-12 ounces cranberries
sprigs of watercress for garnish
strips of orange peel for garnish

Mix the flour, mace and seasoning together. Toss the diced beef in the seasoned flour. Heat the oil in a large pan and brown the beef, in batches. Then transfer to a large flameproof casserole dish. Add the onions, garlic and celery to the pan and sauté for 3-4 minutes, then add mustard and wine. Bring to a boil and reduce for a few minutes. Pour the lot over meat in the casserole. Add the port, stock, herbs and half the cranberries. Cover and cook gently for approximately 2 hours until the meat is tender, or cook in the oven at 375 for about the same time. Fifteen minutes before the end of cooking time, add the remaining cranberries. Check the seasoning before serving and garnish with sprigs of watercress and orange peel.

Recipe courtesy of Bord Bia Irish Food Board

Grottos can be found throughout Ireland, this particular one we
passed on our way to Killybegs. Visitors often leave mementoes.

LET'S TALK for a minute about grocery shopping in Ireland. First of all I have found that the size, (square footage wise), of the grocery store is very deceiving when looking at the storefront. Quite often I have walked into what I believed to be a small store and found that it is 10 times larger than I had anticipated. The storefronts aren't wide but the distance from front to back is, well… a long way to Tipperary! Another interesting tidbit having to do with Irish grocery shopping – the customer supplies the bag or bags for their own groceries. If a shopper doesn't have a bag, one or however many are needed will be supplied, with the bag cost being added to your total. Mother Earth must be very proud of Ireland!

Chicken Casserole with Saffron and Garlic

4 free range chicken breasts
olive oil
2 onions/4 shallots, skin removed and finely
sliced
pinch of salt
3-14-ounce cans organic chickpeas
2 ½ cups chicken or vegetable stock
extra water if needed
6 handfuls baby spinach

black pepper, freshly ground
fresh basil or flat leaf parsley

Bread paste:
3 slices white bread, toasted until golden
2 cloves garlic, chopped
2 tablespoons olive oil
2 large pinches of saffron strands
sea salt

Cut the toasted bread up roughly and pound it to a paste using a pestle and mortar (alternatively, use a food processor). Add the garlic and once the bread and garlic have been almost reduced to paste add the olive oil and the saffron. Continue mixing until the mixture has turned to a fine paste.

Cut each chicken breast into 4 or 5 pieces. Heat some olive oil in a large saucepan and add the onions/shallots with a small pinch of salt to help bring out the juices. Sauté for 2-3 minutes, and add the chicken pieces. Allow chicken to partially cook on each side for a minute or two; add the chickpeas. Stir together and then add the chicken stock. Bring to a boil and reduce heat to a simmer. Cook for a few more minutes, add the spinach. The spinach will reduce quite dramatically. Stir well. Add the bread paste and bring back to a boil, simmer for another 3-4 minutes. Stir in the fresh herbs and serve hot with fresh bread.

Belle Isle School of Cookery
LISBELLAW, ENNISKILLEN
CO. FERMANAGH

Connemara Braised Lamb Shanks

4 lamb shanks, neatly trimmed
2 large onions, peeled and sliced
2 large cloves garlic, crushed and chopped
1-2 tablespoons cooking oil
1 carrot, peeled and sliced
1 stick celery, sliced
1 ¼ cups red wine
14-ounce can of plum tomatoes
1 ¼ cups lamb or beef stock
1 tablespoon red current jelly
large pinch dried mixed herbs, including thyme and rosemary
sea salt, to taste
black pepper, freshly ground to taste

Brown the lamb in a 475 degree oven for 35 minutes. Cook onions and garlic in the oil in a medium-size pan until soft; add the carrots and celery. Add the browned lamb shanks, pour in the red wine and reduce a little. Transfer the mixture from the pan to a casserole dish. Add plum tomatoes, stock, red current jelly, herbs, salt, and pepper. Put lid on casserole dish and place in 225-250 degree oven for 2 ½ hours. Take shanks and vegetables out of sauce, pour sauce into a saucepan and reduce sauce to thicken slightly. Place lamb shanks and vegetables back into the casserole dish and pour the thickened sauce over the top and serve.

Ballywarren Country House
CONG, CO. MAYO

Each year thousands of people stop at Drumcliff Churchyard just outside Sligo Town to visit the grave of the famous poet, William Butler Yeats. My husband Barney stands alongside the grave.

Deviled Scallops

1 ¼ cups milk
8 ounces scallops
2 tablespoons margarine
4 tablespoons flour
1 tablespoon onion, finely chopped
2 tablespoons natural yogurt
1 dessertspoon Worcestershire sauce
1 teaspoon whole grain mustard
1 teaspoon fresh chopped parsley
pinch of cayenne pepper
2 hard boiled eggs, chopped
sea salt to taste
freshly ground black pepper to taste
2 tablespoons Parmesan cheese, grated

Preheat oven to 400 degrees. Place the milk and scallops into a pan. Poach gently for about 3 minutes. Strain the scallops and reserve cooking liquid. Set the scallops aside. Melt the margarine in a pan, stir in the flour and cook 2 minutes. Gradually add the reserved cooking liquid and stir over a gentle heat until the sauce thickens. Remove from the heat and stir in the remaining ingredients, except the Parmesan cheese. Finally fold in the scallops. Sprinkle with Parmesan cheese and bake for 15-20 minutes until golden brown.

Recipe courtesy of Bia na Mara

RUTH AND I LEFT the Belle Isle School of Cookery on a Saturday, the day after our last day of class. During our first week at Belle Isle Ruth had promised to drive me to Dublin to catch my flight home to America. I don't think she realized that I was a little teary-eyed as we traveled down the drive for the last time. We had spent a month together at cookery school, and all of the fond memories were very much in my mind. We would first drive to Belfast, Carrickfergus to be exact, which is home for Ruth. It seems as though we made about three stops before arriving at Ruth's condo, which is smack dab on the water, about 15-20 feet from the marina filled with colorful boats. What a beautiful sight to wake up to! On Sunday morning, around 10 o'clock, we set off on our drive to Dublin. Knowing I wanted to take a few pictures in Belfast, Ruth had an exact itinerary mapped out in her mind. Actually, I think Ruth may well have missed her calling in life, as she is a fabulous tour guide and an excellent driver! We visited Belfast Castle, as well as Queen's University. As we cruised around Ruth pointed out one landmark after another, saving what she knew would be my favorite for last. For years I had wanted to visit the Crown Liquor Saloon, and today was the day. At a quarter to twelve Ruth parked the car, and we quickly hopped out. People were already waiting to go inside. In fifteen minutes we would be inside the place I had visited only through photographs in books. Finally, a man, (thinking back I believe he was one of the bartenders), unlocked the black accordion style metal gate. We were the first people through the gate on that particular Sunday, and we quickly took a couple of stools at the bar. There were loads of people behind us and time was

of the essence. There we were, in the Crown Liquor Saloon, sitting at the bar, looking at the beautiful stained-glass windows from the inside rather than from the outside when the bartender asked, "What can I get for you ladies?" Ruth ordered a soft drink and a bowl of Irish stew, and a huge bowl of Irish stew it was. Now then, normally I wouldn't be drinking one of those dark stouts at twelve o'clock noon, but then again, normally I wouldn't be sitting in one of Northern Ireland's greatest treasures. Perhaps the greatest of all Victorian gin palaces ever. Since it was so early in the day, I thought I should be sensible and order a half-pint rather than a pint, and that is exactly what I did. It wasn't until I drank the half pint that I decided to order the other half. Such a memorable visit!

Ted, Sandy, Linda and John making their way around the 106 miles
in the Ring of Kerry.

Casserole of Kerry Lamb

2 ¼ pound shoulder of lamb, boned and cut into 2-inch cubes
3 tablespoon vegetable oil
2 tablespoons flour
1 teaspoon salt
½ tablespoon black pepper, freshly ground
3 cups water
½ teaspoon crushed, dried rosemary
1 bouquet garni with thyme, rosemary and a bay leaf
8 small potatoes, peeled and sliced
12 button onions weighing about 8 ounces blanched
12 small whole carrots, approximately 1 pound
2 ounces sultanas, (golden colored raisins)
fresh parsley, finely chopped to garnish

Blot all sides of lamb pieces well on absorbent paper towels. Heat the oil in a large heavy based saucepan over medium heat. Add the lamb cubes, a few pieces at a time, and brown on all sides. As the cubes are browned, lift them out of the pan with a slotted spoon and place in a dish to keep warm. When all pieces of lamb are browned, return them to the pan and sprinkle with flour, salt and ground pepper. Toss pieces of meat with a spoon to coat them well. Cook over a moderate heat, stirring occasionally until the flour is lightly browned. Add the water, crushed rosemary and the bouquet garni. Cover the saucepan and bring to a boil. Lower the heat and simmer for 40 minutes. Add the potatoes, onions, carrots, and sultanas. Replace lid and simmer, turning frequently to ensure that the potatoes are covered with liquid. Cook for 45-60 minutes or until the meat is tender and the vegetables are cooked. Adjust seasoning if necessary. Before serving, remove the bouquet garni and skim off the fat. Transfer meat and vegetables to a warm serving dish, pour the stock over, and garnish with finely chopped parsley.

Smugglers Inn
WATERVILLE
CO. KERRY

Guinness & Dumpling Casserole

2 tablespoons oil
1 1/3 pound rib steak, boned, well trimmed and cut into cubes
2 onions, thinly sliced
2 cloves garlic, chopped
1 tablespoon brown sugar
1 tablespoon Odlums Cream Flour (cake flour can be used)
2/3 cup Guinness
2/3 cup water
pinch mixed, dried herbs
1 tablespoon red wine vinegar
1 tablespoon mustard
salt
freshly ground black pepper to taste

Preheat the oven to 325 degrees. Heat the oil in a saucepan. Brown the beef. Remove meat as it browns and place in a 9x9-inch casserole dish. Add the onion and garlic to the saucepan and cook for a few minutes. Sprinkle in the sugar and flour, and stir around to soak up the juices; then gradually add the Guinness and water, continually stirring. Add the dried herbs, wine vinegar, mustard, salt and pepper. Bring to a boil and pour it over the meat in the casserole dish. Cover and bake in oven, for 1 ½ hours, or until the meat is tender. Approximately 30 minutes before the end of cooking time, spoon the dumpling on top of the casserole.

See next page for Dumplings.

Odlums
DUBLIN

Guinness advertisements can be found adorning the many pubs that Ireland is famous for, Howard's Pub is no exception. Never once have I seen a billboard with a Guinness advertisement, billboards are nonexistent in Ireland.

Dumpling ingredients:
1/3 to ½ cup Odlums Self Raising Flour
2 tablespoons chopped fresh parsley
2 tablespoons chopped fresh chives
¼ cup olive oil
¼ cup milk

Mix flour, parsley and chives together in a bowl. Beat milk and oil together and add to dry ingredients forming a soft dough. Drop spoonfuls of dough into casserole an hour before the casserole is finished cooking.

Cottage Pie

1 cup chopped onions
2 tablespoons oil
1 pound cooked minced lamb or mutton
salt and pepper to taste
2-3 drops Worcestershire sauce
1 1/8 cups gravy
1 pound mashed potatoes (made with 2 tablespoons butter and 2 tablespoons milk)
egg-wash or milk to brush on top

Sauté the onion in the oil without coloring. Add the minced lamb or mutton. Season to taste with salt and pepper. Add Worcestershire sauce and enough gravy to bind mixture together. Bring mixture to a boil and simmer for 10 minutes. Put mixture in casserole dish. Spread the mashed potatoes on the top. Make a trellis design in the mashed potatoes with the tines of a fork. Brush with egg-wash or milk. Color lightly under grill. Put remaining gravy in a sauceboat for serving.

*Mushrooms, carrots and sliced tomato with rosemary can be added to the meat mixture
if so desired. The potato topping can include grated cheese.

22 Main Street
KILLYBEGS
CO. DONEGAL

One of the many boats docked in the lively fishing village of Killybegs.

Ham & Cheese Bread Pudding

2 tablespoons butter
1 leek, washed and sliced
8 ounces assorted mushrooms
½ cup dry white wine
salt to taste
freshly ground pepper to taste
1 loaf French bread, cut into 1-inch cubes
½ pound cooked ham, diced

6 ounces (1 ½ cups) Irish cheddar cheese, grated
4 ounces (1 cup) Blarney cheese, grated
2 tablespoons cheddar cheese grated
5 large eggs
2 cups half-and-half
3 teaspoons Dijon mustard
2 tablespoons flat leaf parsley, minced

Lightly butter a 2-quart casserole dish. In a saucepan over medium heat, melt the butter. Add the leeks and cook for 3 minutes, or until tender. Add the mushrooms and cook, stirring frequently, for 2-3 minutes, or until the mushrooms have released their liquid. Stir in the wine and cook, stirring frequently for 5-6 minutes, or until the liquid has nearly evaporated. Season the mixture with salt and pepper. Remove from heat and set aside. Spread half of the bread in the bottom of the prepared dish. Evenly distribute half of the ham and half of the cheeses over the bread. Spread the leeks and mushrooms over the top. Repeat layering with remaining ham and cheeses. In a large bowl, whisk together the eggs, half-and-half, mustard, and parsley. Pour over the bread mixture, cover with plastic wrap, and let stand at room temperature for 30 minutes. Preheat the oven to 350 degrees. Remove the plastic wrap from the pudding and bake for 40 minutes, or until the top is golden brown and the pudding is set. Remove from the oven and let stand for 10 minutes before serving.

Serves 6.

Saint Patrick Centre
DOWN PATRICK
CO. DOWN

THE CENTRE IS an exciting interpretative exhibition which tells the fascinating story of Ireland's Patron Saint. Through Patrick's own words a light is shone on the arrival of Christianity in Ireland and its development through his mission. A series of interactive displays allow visitors to explore how Patrick's legacy developed in early Christian times and reveal the fabulous artwork and metalwork which was produced during this Golden Age. The exhibition also examines the major impact of Irish missionaries in Dark Age Europe—a legacy which remains to this day.

⁂

The altar in the miniature Gothic Cathedral at Kylemore Abbey.

Beef and Guinness Casserole

2 tablespoons oil
2 pounds beef, trimmed and cubed
2 tablespoons tomato puree
1 - 14 ounce can tomatoes, chopped
2 teaspoons mustard
1 tablespoon Worcestershire sauce
½ cup of Guinness
3 ¾ cups chicken stock
pepper to taste
3 carrots, peeled and diced
2 large onions, peeled and sliced
4 mushrooms, sliced
1 teaspoon cornstarch mixed with 1 tablespoon water (optional)
2 tablespoons parsley
boiled potatoes or rice for serving

Heat oil in a large pot, add the meat and cook until brown on all sides. Add the tomato puree, chopped tomatoes, mustard, Worcestershire sauce, Guinness, chicken stock, and pepper; cover with lid and simmer for 20 minutes. Add the vegetables, cover and cook an additional 40-50 minutes until the meat is tender; add cornstarch mixture to thicken if needed. Sprinkle with parsley and serve with boiled potatoes or rice.

Kylemore Abbey & Garden
KYLEMORE, CONNEMARA
CO. GALWAY

Goulash Belleek Style

❦

1-2 tablespoons oil
1 large onion, chopped
1 pounds beef (best cut), cubed *
2 tablespoons flour
2 tablespoons tomato puree
14 ounces can or tin of chopped tomatoes
1 ¼ cups beef stock
1 bay leaf
½ teaspoon caraway seeds
1 red pepper, seeds removed and sliced
1 green pepper, seeds removed and sliced
10 ounces cream
2 tablespoons fresh chopped parsley
cooked potatoes or rice, for serving

Preheat oven to 300 degrees. Put oil in a medium size, heavy pan and fry onion. Coat the cubed meat with flour and add to onion mixture, allowing the meat to brown. Add the tomato puree, chopped tomatoes, beef stock and bay leaf. Mix together and pour into a casserole dish. Place in preheated oven and bake for 30 minutes. Add the caraway seeds and peppers and bake for another 30 minutes. Remove from the oven and allow casserole to cool for about 5 minutes. Add the cream and sprinkle with parsley. Serve with potatoes or rice

*I think everyone would agree that beef tenderloin is the best, but quite pricey.
Other good quality cuts can be used in place of the beef tenderloin.

Belleek Pottery Visitor Centre
BELLEEK
CO. FERMANAGH

Belleek is world famous for the lovely, delicate pottery it produces.

CONGRATULATIONS are in order, as Belleek Pottery, Ireland's oldest pottery, marks its 150th anniversary in 2007. Can you imagine being in business for 150 years? What an achievement ! The Belleek Pottery Visitor Centre expects to welcome over 200,000 visitors to the Center during the anniversary year. The Belleek International Collectors' Convention was held during April and hosted over 400 avid collectors of Belleek china.

Farmers markets are quite popular, particularly leading up to the weekend. I bought my firsst fresh fig ever at this market in Dunglow, Co. Donegal. Figs are pretty, purple, pear-shaped fruits.

Smoked Salmon Bake

⁙

2 pounds potatoes (8-10 average size)
8 ounces smoked salmon, sliced
1 ¼ cups cream
freshly ground black pepper

Preheat the oven to 300 degrees. Peel the potatoes and place in a saucepan. Cover with cold water. Bring potatoes to a boil. Boil 5 minutes. Turn off heat and allow boiling to stop. Drain potatoes. When they are cool enough, cut into slices. Grease an ovenproof dish and arrange a layer of potatoes in the bottom. Next place a layer of smoked salmon and a shaking of pepper. Continue to layer and finish with a layer of potatoes. Pour over the cream and bake in oven for 30-40 minutes.

Odlums
DUBLIN

Baked Hake with Tomato, Herb & Pine Nut Dressing

Small amount of olive oil
2 small onions, finely chopped
1/3 cup pine nuts, roasted
1 teaspoon pesto
6 tomatoes, peeled, seeded and chopped
juice of ½ lemon
1 tablespoon dried mixed herbs, (parsley, dill and chives)
1 cup white wine
salt and pepper
4 hake steaks, about 10 ounces each

Preheat oven to 400 degrees. Place a ceramic dish in the oven to heat. Pour a small amount of olive oil in a small fry pan over a medium heat; add the chopped onions and fry. In a large bowl, combine the fried onions with all the other ingredients, (except the hake steaks), and mix well. Place each hake steak in the ceramic dish that has been heated in the oven. Pour the mixture in the bowl over the hake steaks and bake for about 8 minutes, or until the fish is cooked through.

Ballymakeigh House
KILLEAGH
CO. CORK

WE SPENT A couple of days in Clifden with two other couples from Kentucky - John and Linda from Louisville, Ted and Sandy from Elizabethtown. Clifden is a lively town with loads of activities to keep you occupied, as well as an array of places to visit, and sights to see. It was time to think about dinner and we were trying to decide where to enjoy an evening meal. There is no shortage of restaurants in Clifden, making our decision even more difficult, not to mention choosing a restaurant that all six of us agreed upon. After dinner we were off to a music session at one of the numerous pubs, it was Saturday night and the town was buzzing. With pints in hand, we settled in at our table for a night of music and dance. Strange as it may seem, the majority of the music played was country music; we thought we were back home in Kentucky! Evidently the Irish love country music, and they knew the words to the songs better than we did. When you visit Clifden, keep in mind that the Kylemore Abbey & Garden, and the Dan O'Hara Homestead are in close proximity, and both are well worth the scenic drive. If you were clever in your holiday preparation, your "Heritage Island Essential Touring Guide" is somewhere in your luggage. Use it at just one of the visitor attractions and this informative guide has paid for itself.

Dan's Bacon and Cabbage

❖

1 large cabbage (York is the best)*
8 strips bacon
salt and pepper
4 allspice berries
1 bay leaf
1 ¼ cups bacon or chicken stock
baked potatoes for serving

Cut the cabbage in half and boil for 15 minutes in salted water. Drain cabbage, and soak in cold water for 1 minute; then drain well and slice. Line the bottom of a casserole with half the bacon strips, then put the cabbage on top and add the seasonings. Add enough stock to barely cover; then put the remaining strips of bacon on top. Cover and simmer for one hour on stovetop, until most of the liquid is absorbed. Serve with baked potatoes.

*York cabbage is hard to come by in America. I substitute Savoy cabbage.

Dan O'Hara Homestead
CLIFDEN, CONNEMARA
CO. GALWAY

Dan O'Hara's Heritage & History Centre
Photo courtesy of Heritage Island

❧

IF YOU FIND yourself in the Connemara region of Ireland, which is in the West, why not visit one of Ireland's top tourist attractions? Dan O'Hara Heritage and History Centre is an award-winning visitor attraction nestled into a hillside just below the Twelve Bens, (a mountain range). Dan O'Hara was a 19th century Irish tenant farmer. Here you will find a working farm that will give you a unique insight as to what farm life was like in the pre-famine days. Take a look at the restored cottage of Dan O'Hara and try to imagine what life would have been like in those long gone days. If you have ever heard talk of the peat bogs of Ireland, this would be a perfect place to see a bog. One of Dan O'Hara's descendents will gladly show you around.

Fergus View Lamb Casserole

1 medium onion, chopped
1 clove garlic, crushed and chopped
1-2 tablespoons oil
1 pound pieces of stewing lamb
1 pound carrots, peeled and cut into 1-inch pieces
½ pound celery, cut into 1-inch pieces
14-ounce can of whole tomatoes
1 tablespoon fresh rosemary, chopped
1 tablespoon fresh marjoram, chopped
1 tablespoon fresh parsley, chopped
½ teaspoon granulated mustard
1 tablespoon organic honey
1 orange, segmented
1 chicken stock cube
2 2/3 cups water
freshly cracked pepper
rosemary sprigs to garnish

Lightly sauté chopped onion and garlic in oil. Add lamb pieces and cook until browned. Add the carrots, celery, tomatoes, all chopped herbs, mustard, honey and orange segments, stir. Dissolve the chicken stock cube in the water and sprinkle with pepper. Bring to a simmer. Transfer to an ovenproof dish and place in oven for 1 ½ to 2 hours. Garnish with fresh rosemary sprigs.

Fergus View Guesthouse
KILNABOY, COROFIN
CO. CLARE

Spiced Beef & Orange Casserole

❧

1 large onion, diced
2 tablespoons oil
6 ounces mushrooms, quartered
1 ½ pounds stewing steak, cubed
1 ½ ounces plain flour
1 ¼ cups beef stock
1 ¼ cups orange juice
2 teaspoons wine vinegar
2 teaspoons soft brown sugar
1 cinnamon stick
1 bouquet garni made up with fresh parsley, thyme and a bay leaf
grated orange rind
salt and pepper
1 tablespoon dark rum
new potatoes, rice or pasta for serving
garnish: sour cream, chives and blanched orange rind

Preheat oven to 375 degrees. Sauté the onion in the oil. Add the mushrooms and beef; cook until the meat is brown. Add the flour and cook for 1 minute, stirring continuously. Gradually add stock and orange juice. Stir in remaining ingredients, (except dark rum), and bring to a boil. Transfer to a casserole dish and cook for 2-2 ½ hours. Remove the bouquet garni and stir in the rum. Serve with new potatoes, rice or pasta. Top with the garnish.

De Barra's
CLONAKILTY
WEST CORK

DE BARRA'S HOLDS quite a few impressive awards. It seems that De Barra's is tops in whatever they set out to accomplish. In 1984 De Barra's won its first National Award, Bord Na Gaeilge National Shop Front Award Winner, which took place during the Tidy Towns Competition. De Barra's also holds a few Dining Awards, as well as the Black & White Pub of the Year Award for 2004. There is even an award for being an authentic Irish Pub in 2001: it is the James Joyce Pub Award. De Barra's was also selected in 2002 for the Traditional Irish Music Pub of the year. If you don't have Clonakilty, West Cork on your itinerary you would be wise to add it in, and stop at De Barra's for a meal, a pint and some good music. It will be an experience you will never forget.

Michael & Mary's Pot Roast Pheasant

1 tablespoon olive oil
1 tablespoon butter
1 plump pheasant, cleaned, cut in half, soaked in salted water, and patted dry
salt and pepper, to taste
6 shallots, sliced or chopped
1/2 red pepper, seeded and cut into strips
1/2 yellow pepper, seeded and cut into strips
1 fresh sprig of thyme
1 bay leaf
3 tablespoons Calvados (apple brandy)
3 cups sweet cider
1 pound small, firm button mushrooms
1 teaspoon flour
1 teaspoon butter
rice for serving

In a large skillet heat olive oil and butter over a medium heat until butter is melted. Add the pheasant halves and brown until they become golden in color on all sides. Remove breasts from pan and place them in a large Dutch oven, (breast sides up). Season the pheasant halves with salt and pepper. Add the shallots, red and yellow pepper to the skillet and sauté, adding a little more butter and olive oil, (do not allow to cook completely). Add mixture in skillet to the pheasant halves along with the sprig of thyme and bay leaf. Pour the Calvados into a small saucepan and warm it, then ignite with a match. Pour the flaming Calvados over the pheasant, wait a minute or so and pour in the sweet cider. Place the Dutch oven on a stovetop burner and bring everything to a very low simmer. Cover with lid and simmer for 1 hour and 15 minutes or until tender. During the last 20 minutes of cooking time add the button mushrooms. Check during cooking time to make sure there is enough liquid to keep the meat from drying out. Add more cider if necessary. When done remove pheasant halves, shallots, peppers and mushrooms to a warmed serving plate. Discard the herbs, then boil the liquid in the Dutch oven until it has reduced slightly. Mix the teaspoon of flour into the 1 teaspoon of butter to make a paste. Add paste to reduced liquid and whisk to thicken. Remove sauce from heat and use to pour over pheasant and vegetables when serving. Serve over rice.

Michael Kennedy Ceramics
GORT, CO. GALWAY
SLIGO TOWN, CO. SLIGO

❧

I HAVE BEEN COLLECTING Michael Kennedy Pottery for the past 9 years, buying various pieces during each of my Irish holidays. Michael has a workshop and a retail shop in Gort, Co. Galway, and a new retail shop in Sligo Town. I have spent time in each location trying to decide exactly what I need (want) to take home with me. Such a difficult choice, this you will understand when you visit. His designs are quite unique and there is a great assortment of colors and styles to choose from, the pottery will surely dazzle you!

A small grouping of Michael's creativity.

Pork in a Crust

1 ½ pounds pastry
2 tablespoons sugar
dash nutmeg
dash salt
dash pepper
6 thick slices pork loin
2 apples, peeled, cored and sliced
2 cups white wine
2 tablespoons butter

Preheat oven to 375 degrees. Roll out half of the pastry and line the bottom of a pie dish. Mix the sugar, nutmeg, salt and pepper together. Arrange alternate layers of pork and apples in the pastry. Sprinkle each layer with the sugar mixture. Add the wine and dot with butter. Roll out the remaining pastry crust and place on top of pork and apple mixture. Bake for 45-50 minutes.

Palace Stables & Heritage Centre
ARMAGH CITY
CO. ARMAGH

Photo courtesy of Heritage Island

Smoked Salmon & Potato Gratin

⁛

2 pounds cooked potatoes, sliced
black pepper, freshly ground
fresh chives, chopped
8 ounces smoked salmon, sliced very thin, and cut into thin strips
juice of half a lemon
1 cup fresh milk
1 cup fresh cream
2 tablespoons butter

Preheat the oven to 400 degrees. Butter a deep round oven-proof dish. Arrange thinly sliced potatoes in a layer, adding black pepper and chives. Arrange smoked salmon pieces in strips on top of the potatoes and sprinkle with lemon juice. Repeat this layering until dish is almost full. Mix milk into cream and pour the mixture over the top. Place dabs of butter on the top and bake in the oven for 30 minutes.

*A nice salad of rocket lettuce, red onions, toasted almonds and a warm vinaigrette dressing goes down well with this dish.

Recipe courtesy of Bia na Mara

Durrus & Potato Melt

2 pounds waxy potatoes, cubed
2 onions, finely chopped
2 tablespoons butter
½ pound bacon slices cut into small pieces
1 pound Durrus Farmhouse Cheese, rind removed and cut into cubes*
8-ounce tub of crème fraiche
butter, enough to butter an oven-proof dish
salt and pepper to taste

Preheat oven to 350 degrees. Parboil the potatoes and set aside. Gently cook the onions in the butter, add the bacon and cook in a covered pan until onions are soft and bacon is cooked. Mix the cubed Durrus Farmhouse cheese, cream fraiche and potatoes together; add the onion and bacon mixture in and pour into a buttered oven-proof dish. Sprinkle with salt and pepper to taste. Place in preheated oven and bake for 15-20 minutes, stirring gently half way through cooking.

*Durrus Farmhouse Cheese is available at Whole Foods Markets as well as other gourmet cheese stores.

*The people of Durrus Farmhouse cheese suggest serving this lovely casserole with a green salad, and a cracking bottle of wine of your choice; it is equally good with red or white.

Durrus Farmhouse Cheese
COOMKEEN, DURRUS
WEST CORK

IT WAS RAINING BUCKETS when Kathryn met Ruth and me in Dublin. It was the day before I was to wing my way back to America. Just as she had promised one month earlier, Ruth had driven me to Dublin. I was anxious to see my family after my six-week Irish holiday. First though, I would spend the night with Kathryn, one of my cookery school comrades and a roommate, as well. Kathryn and her husband Nigel live but a stones throw from the Famous K Club in Straffan, Co. Kildare. Just a couple of short weeks prior we wouldn't have been able to drive anywhere near the K Club, as the Ryder Cup was in full swing. But tonight we passed easily. Kathryn prepared a lovely dinner, incorporating a few of our "Belle Isle School of Cookery" recipes into the menu. Everything was fabulous! Soon we turned in for the night, as we had a full schedule the next day. As I tossed and turned, trying to fall asleep, I thought back to the day Barney and I had arrived for our Irish Holiday. The days had absolutely flown by.

Flags proudly displayed at the famous K Club. During the 2006 Ryder Cup.

My classmates at the Belle Isle School of Cookery. I am in the center
holding a handful of forks.

Poule au Pot (French Chicken Casserole)

4 tablespoons butter
1 tablespoon olive oil
6 thick slices smoked bacon, cut into ½ inch
by 1-inch pieces
1 free range chicken
sea salt
black pepper, freshly milled
4 cups water
1 ¼ cups wine
3 sprigs fresh tarragon

6 cloves
4 cloves garlic, peeled but left whole
2 bay leaves
8-10 medium potatoes, peeled and
quartered
4 carrots, peeled and cut into batons
3 parsnips, peeled and cut into batons
3 leeks, well washed and sliced
4 medium onions, peeled and quartered
handfull of freshly chopped parsley

Preheat the oven to 350 degrees. On the stovetop, in a large Dutch oven melt the butter with the olive oil. Add the lardoons of bacon and cook for 2-3 minutes over a medium heat. Season the chicken with the sea salt and pepper, and place in the Dutch oven. Add the water and wine along with the fresh tarragon sprigs, cloves, garlic and bay leaves. Bring to a boil, remove from the stovetop and place in the oven for 40 minutes. Remove from the oven and add the potatoes, carrots, parsnips, leeks and onion quarters. Place back in the oven for an additional 25 minutes. Remove from the oven and stir in the chopped parsley. Season again, with sea salt and freshly milled black pepper. Remove the chicken and carve for serving. Serve in deep bowls with crusty bread.

Belle Isle School of Cookery
LISBELLAW, ENNISKILLEN
CO. FERMANAGH

WHEN TOURING IRELAND make sure to include a few of the Heritage towns listed below, they are lovely. The towns and villages included on the list are all memorable places to visit. There is an array of reasons these towns have the distinction of being designated as "Heritage Towns". All are steeped in history, and each has its own unique character. Do you know that Cobh was the last port of call for the Titanic? Kinsale is one of Ireland's most charming ports, with narrow streets winding through the village and numerous restaurants for your dining pleasures. The architecture in Youghal is in a class of its own. I could go on and on, but really, you just need to find your way to Ireland and see for yourself, and you will see why I wake up and fall to sleep thinking about Ireland.

Birr, Co. Offaly
Cashel, Co. Tipperary
Cobh, Co. Cork
Dalkey, Co. Dublin
Kell, Co. Meath
Killaloe/Ballina, Co. Clare/Tipperary
Kilrush, Co. Clare
Kinsale, Co. Cork
Lismore, Co. Waterford
Listowel, Co. Kerry
Tipperary, Co. Tipperary
Trim, Co. Meath
Westport, Co. Mayo
Youghal, Co. Cork

Celtic crosses or high crosses can be found throughout Ireland.
This one looked absolutely perfect with the ever-so-blue water
in the background.

Contributors

The Apple Farm, Cahir, Co. Tipperary

Ashford Castle, Cong, Co. Mayo

Avondale House & Forest Park, Rathdrum, Co. Wicklow

Ballymakeigh House, Killeagh, Co. Cork

Ballywarren Country House, Cong, Co. Mayo

Belle Isle School of Cookery, Lisbellaw, Enniskillen, Co. Fermanagh

Belleek Pottery Visitor Centre, Belleek, Co. Fermanagh

Bia na Mara

Bord Bia Irish Food Board

The Boulevard Guest House, Westport, Co. Mayo

Bunratty Castle & Folk Park, Bunratty, Co. Clare

Charleville Lodge, Dublin

Connemara Smokehouse, Ballyconneely, Co. Galway

The Curragh Racecourse, Co. Kildare

Dan O'Hara Homestead, Clifden, Connemara, Co. Galway

De Barra's, Clonakilty, West Cork

Dovecot Restaurant at Adare Heritage Centre, Adare, Co. Limerick

Drumcreehy Guest House, Ballyvaughn, Co. Clare

Durrus Farmhouse Cheese, Coomkeen, Durrus, West Cork

Egan's House, Dublin City

Farney Castle, Holycross, Co. Tipperary

Fergus View, Kilnaboy, Corofin, Co. Clare

Fitzpatrick's Bar & Restaurant, Dundalk, Co. Louth

Florence Court, Enniskillen, Co. Fermanagh

Gleeson's Townhouse & Restaurant, Roscommon Town, Co. Roscommon

Guinness Storehouse, Dublin

J&L Grubb Ltd

Kilcoran Lodge Hotel, Cahir, Co. Tipperary

Kylemore Abbey & Garden, Kylemore, Connemara, Co. Galway

Michael Kennedy Ceramics, Gort, Co. Galway and Sligo Town, Co. Sligo

Murphy Brewery, Cork, Co. Cork

Odlums

O'Doherty's, Enniskillen, Co. Fermanagh

Palace Stables Heritage Centre, Armagh City, Co. Armagh

Park Hotel Kenmare, Kenmare, Co. Kerry

Rathsallagh House Hotel & Golf Club, Dunlavin, Co. Wicklow

Saint Patrick Centre, Down Patrick, Co. Down

St. Clerans Manor House, Craughwell, Co. Galway

Scoffs Restaurant, Enniskillen, Co. Fermanagh

Smugglers Inn, Waterville, Co. Kerry

Stonebridge Restaurant, Richhill, Co. Armagh

Strokestown Park, Strokestown, Co. Roscommon

22 Main Street Restaurant, Killybegs, Co. Donegal

ORDERING THE "Essential Touring Guide" from Heritage Island was the single, most sensible move I made in planning our most recent adventure in Ireland. Included in the guide are Visitor Attractions and Heritage Towns throughout Northern Ireland and the Republic of Ireland, all right there at your fingertips. There are numerous places to visit. Castles, museums, gardens, forts and various houses, all well worth including on your itinerary. Our mistake was that we didn't take full advantage of visiting more places. So, it's back to the drawing board, to plan another holiday in the Emerald Isle. We will just have to pick up where we left off. Use the "Essential Touring Guide" just once and it has more than paid for itself. What more can you ask?

**Celtic cross in front of Parish Church of St. Malachy located in the
pretty Georgian village of Hillsborough, Co. Down.**

Save over $500
at Ireland's Top Visitor Attractions!

With concise information on over 80 of Ireland's Leading Visitor Attractions and Heritage Towns, the Essential Touring Guide to Ireland's Visitor Attractions is ideal for anyone touring the Emerald Isle. Worth over $500 in potential savings, simply present the Guide at any of the featured venues to receive discounts on admission and other special offers.

Pidgeon's Press readers can get 50% off the price of the Essential Touring Guide. Fill in the form below and post or fax to Heritage Island along with your credit card details, and we will send you your copy of the Guide for just EUR2.99.

Name:	Card Type:
Address:	Number:
Country:	Expiry date:
No. of Guides:	Security Number:

Mail to: Heritage Island, Marina House, 11-13 Clarence Street, Dun Laoghaire, Co. Dublin, Ireland. Tel: +353 1 236 6890 Fax: +353 1 236 6895

Index